Presented To:

_____

From:

_____

Date:

_____

SPIRITUAL
A.D.D.

SPIRITUAL A.D.D.

OVERCOMING SPIRITUAL ATTENTION DEFICIT DISORDER

HANK KUNNEMAN

DESTINY IMAGE® PUBLISHERS, INC.

P.O. Box 310, Shippensburg, PA 17257-0310

"Promoting Inspired Lives"

This book and all other Destiny Image, Revival Press, MercyPlace, Fresh Bread, Destiny Image Fiction, and Treasure House books are available at Christian bookstores and distributors worldwide.

For a U.S. bookstore nearest you, call 1-800-722-6774.

For more information on foreign distributors, call 717-532-3040.

Reach us on the Internet: www.destinyimage.com.

ISBN 13 TP: 978-0-7684-3967-0

ISBN 13 Ebook: 978-0-7684-8935-4

For Worldwide Distribution, Printed in the U.S.A.

1 2 3 4 5 6 7 8 9 10 11 / 13 12 11

DEDICATION

This book is dedicated to those who are honest
enough to say that at times they have struggled with
Spiritual A.D.D.

CONTENTS

INTRODUCTION

I never thought about writing a book on Spiritual A.D.D. before. In fact, I didn't really even quite know if there was such a thing. It wasn't until I heard an advertisement on television describing people with the symptoms of what is commonly known as A.D.D., or attention deficit disorder, that I began to realize that a similar experience can affect people spiritually. I started to notice the symptoms described on television in people I counseled, such as loss of attention, restlessness, difficulty focusing, distractions, disorganization, a wandering mind, boredom, tiredness, and the like. I started to draw many parallels between A.D.D. and Spiritual A.D.D.

The thought soon occurred to me, *I need to write a book that helps people who are dealing with these spiritual symptoms in their Christian walk.* I always like to help people and especially connect them to God. I thought writing a book like this would be such an easy task—was I wrong! Though I have authored several books before, I have never had a more difficult time putting together what I thought would be a simple manuscript. I was dealing with Spiritual A.D.D. myself in trying to write it. In fact, even the way this manuscript was written is different from how I normally write. I was writing a little in each chapter, skipping around, and struggling with a mountain of distractions. However, in the end, I believe I have put together a life-changing book that will help many!

As you read this book you will be challenged to examine yourself and get honest. It will make you laugh, possibly cry, and I am prepared if you decide to get angry and throw the book. Yet, if you stay with the journey through these pages, your spiritual life with God will deepen in an amazing way.

What I didn't realize until I began to pen the pages of this manuscript was how much in my own life, in over 25 years of serving God and nearly as many in the ministry, I too have dealt with the symptoms of Spiritual A.D.D. from time to time. I always like to write from experiences, sharing real life stories, whether they are mine or someone else's. I pray you, the reader, will find that refreshing and encouraging as you examine your life regarding whether Spiritual A.D.D. has a grip on you. Go ahead; start turning the pages. I believe when you reach this book's final page, you will be glad you did!

Chapter One

TAKING THE EXAM

Let us examine our ways and test them, and let us return to the LORD (Lamentations 3:40 NIV).

"I am not going to pray, read my Bible, worship, or even try to stir myself up today," I said, letting God know I how felt. I was feeling weary, distracted, and overwhelmed, and I just plain old did not want to do anything spiritual. Sound familiar? I was determined that when I went to have time with God that day I wasn't going to do anything; I just couldn't. My intention was not to sound mad at God, to look for a reason to not talk with Him, or to be a brat. Rather, my heart was crying out to God because I really needed Him and felt so disconnected.

SPIRITUAL A.D.D.

I continued my speech to Him. "I am going to lie here on the ground and not do anything!" What!? Is that a good idea? Certainly this should not be the norm when it comes to spending time with God or spiritual things. I continued, "I am not doing anything, Lord, but rather I am expecting You to speak a word to me, sing to me, strengthen me, and when I get up from this floor, I will be refreshed!"

Do you know what happened? I fell asleep, snoring, slobbering, lying face down with my head buried in the carpet. I awakened soon after and didn't sense anything different, so I lay there some more and fell asleep again. I was determined not to do anything but let it be God's turn to minister to me. Thank the Lord that He did help me, strengthen me, and minister to me that day! I woke up refreshed and then realized there had been a subtle pattern in my life for a few months. Little did I know that I had been suffering from what I would call spiritual attention deficit disorder or Spiritual A.D.D.

This story describes the struggle that I had been having in my prayer life and spiritual life at that time. If most people, even preachers, were to be honest, they would admit they have struggled with this at times as well. I have a great relationship with the Lord and seek Him diligently; however, my goal in writing on this subject is to be transparent with you in order to help anyone who may be dealing with Spiritual A.D.D.

Symptoms of Spiritual A.D.D.

You may be asking yourself, *What are the symptoms of Spiritual A.D.D., and do I have it?* In order to understand if this problem is in your life, you need to know the symptoms. Recognizing the symptoms is pretty easy since Spiritual A.D.D. has many of the same symptoms as the well-known medical condition of A.D.D., only in a spiritual sense. Could there really be something like A.D.D. that can affect you spiritually in much the same way? Yes, absolutely! And it can be treated when recognized. You will find out in this book how to recognize the symptoms and what to do if you have been affected.

We know that A.D.D. is not a laughing matter and that it affects many people today. Neither is Spiritual A.D.D., and it is affecting many Christians. To help you better understand the spiritual symptoms, I am going to look at the natural symptoms of A.D.D. and draw spiritual parallels.

Some common things that begin to happen in our spiritual lives that may indicate we are being affected by Spiritual A.D.D. are forgetfulness, feelings of distraction, and inability to fight distraction. We may struggle with poor concentration or start to procrastinate, failing to finish what we have started. We may also become more and more disorganized. These are just a few things that could indicate we may need to address our spiritual lives.

SPIRITUAL A.D.D.

To better help you understand, I have included a more complete list of symptoms of A.D.D. These are often the key symptoms of a medically diagnosed case of A.D.D. and can be applied to Spiritual A.D.D. as well.

- Distractions

- Difficulty concentrating

- Disorganization

- Difficulty focusing and paying attention

- Forgetfulness

- Problems following directions

- Procrastination

- Difficulty finishing projects

- Restlessness (feeling fidgety and antsy)

- Problems with time management and lateness

- Misplacement of things and difficulty remembering

- Racing thoughts and a wandering mind

- Frequent boredom

- Mood swings

- Lack of self control[1]

This list of A.D.D. symptoms, though not comprehensive, can help you better identify what may be happening in your spiritual life. It also can help you recognize what might be causing frustration, struggle, or boredom concerning the things of God.

Drawing Parallels

Many parallels can be drawn as to how our spiritual lives can be affected by looking at the symptoms of A.D.D. Even though A.D.D. isn't usually associated with spiritual life, it can cross over to affect our spiritual lives if we let it. These symptoms of A.D.D. can render us spiritually ineffective, making us frustrated, bored, tired, and spiritually sloppy.

Let's look at the list again, comparing it to our spiritual lives:

Distractions

Difficulty concentrating

Difficulty focusing and paying attention

Restlessness (feeling fidgety and antsy)

Racing thoughts and a wandering mind

We may have experienced these things when praying. If we are having difficulty concentrating, our mind wanders and we struggle to find the words to pray. We might find ourselves watching the clock or moving around in a restless, fidgety, or antsy manner. When reading the Bible, our minds might tend to wander, so we don't really comprehend what we are reading. We may start praying or pursuing the things of God, but we stop because we would rather do something else and we find it hard to focus on God. If so, we let distractions get the better of us.

Disorganization

Forgetfulness

Procrastination

Difficulty finishing projects

This may be the case in our spiritual lives if we can never seem to find time for God and God's time is often replaced with something else less important. Do we let the busyness of life cause us to be disorganized, resulting in little to no regular time with God? We might start one day determining to make God and His spiritual things a priority, but soon procrastination sets in until spiritual things are almost non-existent. This can result in self-condemnation and frustration, which make it difficult to finish or continue.

Problems following directions

Problems with time management and lateness

Misplacement of things and difficulty remembering

The busyness of our lives and the lack of spiritual focus may start to affect our spiritual lives, our convictions, and how we conduct ourselves as Christians. If so, we may no longer see a need to defend or uphold the things we once stood for. This can happen when we aren't following the directions of Scripture and aren't seeking first His Kingdom and His righteousness. We may struggle with our daily devotions and daily walk simply because our time management isn't putting God first at the beginning of the day and in all things.

Slowly, over time, we can become more and more forgetful of God, and our hearts can grow cold and distant from Him. When this happens, a change takes place in our spiritual walk—in how we should be living as one sold out to the Lord and His purposes. If we find ourselves constantly misplacing our Bibles, it is probably because we aren't reading God's Word or making a point to make it a priority in our lives.

SPIRITUAL A.D.D.

Boredom comes easily

Mood swings

Lack of self control

It is important to ask ourselves, *Is my spiritual life becoming boring and mundane? Does it lack attention and self control? Do I have to muster up the feeling to pray, read the Bible, or go to church?* If we aren't careful, we might have mood swings and fleshly attitudes, resulting in our flesh overruling our spirits. This is not implying that occasional boredom or the need to control our flesh is Spiritual A.D.D. Rather, these are indicators of Spiritual A.D.D. when they are a frequent occurrence (or are increasing in frequency).

I hope you are beginning to see how the list of the natural symptoms often identified with A.D.D parallels Spiritual A.D.D., which may be hindering your spiritual life and growth. I am not claiming to be a medical doctor or an expert on the condition of A.D.D. But I can look at my own life and what I have dealt with at times regarding distractions in spiritual things, spiritual boredom, difficulty concentrating on the things of God, and spiritual tiredness, just to name a few. Many simple truths and parallels between A.D.D. and Spiritual A.D.D. can be drawn by considering the list.

Of course, people who have been diagnosed with A.D.D. don't necessarily have Spiritual A.D.D. The converse is also true. If people have these symptoms in their spiritual lives, they should not assume they have A.D.D. and need to be diagnosed as such. This comparison is simply to get you to examine yourself and look at the possible source of the things hindering or frustrating you in your pursuit of a rewarding spiritual life with God.

Now it's time to take the exam. It is a healthy and necessary test to determine if you need to address and treat this condition in your spiritual life. The key is to be willing to examine yourself.

The Self-Exam

For some of us it may not be easy to admit we could have Spiritual A.D.D. or even be willing to examine ourselves to determine our spiritual condition. However, Scripture says that we are to examine ourselves as a part of our Christian walk. *"Examine yourselves, whether ye be in the faith; prove your own selves…"* (2 Cor. 13:5). An important place to start in overcoming Spiritual A.D.D. is self-examination; it helps us to recognize the symptoms and keeps us on a healthier path in our walk with God.

A self-examination begins with your heart—your heart attitude and approach to things. Are you giving God your best? What is your approach to the things of God? Are you excited or bored? Then you should examine your overall fruit, or results, in your walk with God. Are you going through the motions, or are you enjoying the benefits of a productive walk with God? Make a list noting certain behaviors, patterns, and attitudes that may be plaguing your spiritual walk. How much time are you investing in your spiritual life? To what level are you growing, or are you struggling to keep your spiritual life alive? Once symptoms are identified, you need to begin to deal with them (you will learn how to do that as you proceed through this book). Remember, whatever the case may be, you must being willing to examine your life and heart in order to produce the best results in the end.

When I was in school, I learned the hard way the importance of self-examination and the necessity of staying on the right path and not getting distracted. I'll never forget the day we went hiking through deep woods on a field trip. It was exciting and full of adventure! As a class, we were told to stay on the path and stay with the group, which for the most part I did—except for a few occasions when some of my friends would wander into the woods, just a little off the path, at certain stops. At times I would join them to do more exploring. But I was also being mindful to stay with the group and the boring—I mean *boring*—guide.

It seemed that our guide would stop every few feet and give us a lengthy speech, reminding us to stay on the path due to poison ivy and ticks. The problem with that was that we were getting distracted, losing focus, and becoming just plain bored. So, we decided to do what we wanted, which led to us not listening very well. We thought that as long as we were in earshot and could still see the group we would be fine. At the end of the day, we were told to examine ourselves to make sure we didn't have poison ivy or ticks.

Guess what? Everyone who was diligent to stay on the path was fine, but those of us who wandered off the path from time to time weren't. I wound up with ticks, and my friends got poison ivy. It was all because we got off the path and started wandering and not following directions. We should have paid attention, listened, and stayed on the path; then we wouldn't have had to deal with ticks and poison ivy!

Self-examination of our hearts and the paths we were choosing would have helped us avoid those problems, which we brought upon ourselves. In the same way, we all need to self-examine our hearts and spiritual condition. We must stay on the path of the Bible and spiritual pursuit of God and righteousness. When we don't listen to God and keep His ways, we get distracted and bored, and we will suffer consequences that aren't pleasant to our spiritual lives, like my friends and I did that day with the ticks and poison ivy.

This is because disobedience also opens our lives up to the enemy—who works to kill, steal, and destroy our spiritual walk, getting us off our spiritual path. This is exactly what Spiritual A.A.D. is intended to do in our lives, which is why the devil loves it. In fact, he is known as one of Spiritual A.D.D.'s biggest fans and perpetrators. He uses it to distract, frustrate, and remove us from our path of spiritual pursuit and satisfaction with God.

However, when you do your best to stay on a dedicated path of spiritual pursuit, you are less likely to fall into the enemy's traps. You are also less likely to develop things that can make your life miserable, like the ticks and poison ivy. Self-examination of your heart, spiritual condition, and life will help you to better identify the symptoms you are dealing with so that you can be helped.

To help further determine the quality of your spiritual life and to identify and overcome symptoms that may be trying to hinder you, ask yourself the questions below. Remember, Spiritual A.D.D. is a condition that can result in many spiritual challenges and problems, so it is important to answer these questions honestly. The self-examination of your heart and spiritual life is not only healthy, but God requires and expects it.

1. How often do you start to pray, read the Bible, or go to church and then quit?

2. Is it difficult for you to organize and stay consistent with spiritual things?

3. How often do you have problems remembering God, your daily devotions, prayer, and Bible reading?

4. When spiritual tasks require effort, do you avoid or delay them?

5. How often do you get fidgety or squirm during church or spiritual devotions?

6. Do you have difficulty paying attention to spiritual things?

7. Are you having mood changes about spiritual things, feeling interest in them one day and becoming uninterested the next?

8. Do you have physical symptoms—such as tiredness, poor sleep, or low energy and concentration—that are making it difficult to focus on spiritual things?

9. Are you having trouble managing your spiritual life?

How did you do on this self-examination? Did you find yourself relating to any of these questions? If you answered yes, it is probably a good indication that you may be falling prey to Spiritual A.D.D.

The Waters of Self-Examination

We are going to look at some helpful truths now regarding the tabernacle that Moses built and how it relates it to the New Testament Church today and our spiritual lives. In the Old Testament, God gave instruction to Moses to build a tabernacle for Him, which is referenced many times in Scripture. One of the first things that God required of those entering this tabernacle was that they look in a basin of water and cleanse themselves. This was because God wanted their *undivided attention* and focus *without the distractions* of this world that could affect their time with Him. Even though this practice was for the priests before they could go any farther into the presence of God, it applies to us prophetically as believers. We are now called kings and priests unto God who must examine our hearts in a similar way if we are to go deeper into the Lord's presence (see Rev. 1:6).

The basin was called the brazen laver and was made with material of shiny brass in which the priests could see their reflection. The reason it was set in the outer court, by God, was for the purpose of self-examination.

> *They made the bronze basin and its bronze stand from the mirrors of the women who served at the entrance to the Tent of Meeting* (Exodus 38:8 NIV).

As they would come to the laver, they would see a reflection of themselves and would wash their hands and feet with the water. They did this before proceeding farther into His presence, into the places in the tabernacle called the inner court and the holy of holies.

> *Then the LORD said to Moses, "Make a bronze basin, with its bronze stand, for washing. Place it between the Tent of Meeting and the altar, and put water in it. Aaron and his sons are to wash their hands and feet with water from it. Whenever they enter the Tent of Meeting, they shall wash with water so that they will not die. Also, when they approach the altar to minister by presenting an offering made to the LORD by fire, they shall wash their hands and feet so that they will not die...* (Exodus 30:17-21 NIV).

Did you notice the seriousness of this laver and self-examination? They were told twice by God that they were to wash themselves or die. This is much like today: Some are dying spiritually because they won't take a hard (but not condemning) look at themselves and the state of their Christian lives.

This is exactly what Jesus referred to when He told a story about a Pharisee who would pray self-righteous prayers, boasting of his own righteousness, while judging the acts of others. He refused to examine himself. In the same story, Jesus spoke of another man, a tax collector and sinner, who self-examined his heart, motives, and lifestyle, beating his breast and asking for God's mercy and forgiveness (see Luke 18:9-14). The point

Jesus was making with the story is that people often will point out the faults in others but won't examine their own lives.

Again, with this in mind, the brazen laver can be prophetically applied to us today, indicating the need that we all have to examine ourselves to make sure we are living as we should before Almighty God! We have to look at ourselves today, washing our hands and feet spiritually through self-examination. Why the hands and feet? Because the hands speak prophetically of our service and work for God that must be clean. The feet prophetically represent a clean walk before God that is focused and purposeful.

Self-examination is also a necessary step if we are going enjoy a life that pursues God in a deeper and more intimate way. We have to be willing to look at ourselves, our hearts, and our spiritual condition. Failure to do this is what often causes us to fall prey to Spiritual A.D.D.

The more honest you are with yourself about the state of your spiritual condition, the more easily you will rid your life of the symptoms. Are you examining your hands to serve God fully? Are you truly walking in a manner pleasing to Him with full dedication?

I have found the more I am honest with myself as to my heart and approach to God and spiritual things, the more easily I resist the symptoms of Spiritual A.D.D. I do this by making myself pursue God, read my Bible, pray, and go to church, regardless of how I feel. I keep myself in an attitude and approach to life that is full of joy when it comes to God. Pursuing Him is not something I am being forced to do but what I want to do; it is what I enjoy doing! Remember, it is the joy of the Lord that is your strength, and in the presence of God there is the fullness of joy (see Neh. 8:10; Ps. 16:11).

This is why it is important to get honest and face yourself, like the priests did when they looked into the brazen laver. It keeps Spiritual A.D.D. from taking root in your life. It is important to do a regular self-examination and spiritual checkup to keep you from sliding backward into a spiritual state that becomes unproductive and frustrating. It also breaks the enemy's ability to use Spiritual A.D.D. in your life.

God requires us to self-examine, to inspect and keep our spiritual lives in order. It is our responsibility to do a spiritual checkup and resist the things that want to hinder and affect our spiritual walk in a negative way. God is waiting on us to see what is in our hearts. He is looking to see how we will deal with the things that are allowing Spiritual A.D.D. to take root in our lives.

This is what the Lord did with Gideon and his army in Judges 7. He wanted to see what was in their hearts and what level of spiritual commitment they had. Did they trust the Lord to fight for them? One of the ways God did this was similar to the brazen laver used in Moses' tabernacle. God once again used water as a reflection of self-examination to cause them to be tested. He made them look into the water and face themselves. It would later reveal something that was missing in their lives in order to win the battle they were about to face. This water of testing would ultimately reveal their true hearts and focus. He separated those who were distracted from those who were focused and determined in order to enable them to defeat the enemy.

Israel had 32,000 men to fight with Gideon against the Midianites, whom the Bible says were as numerous as grasshoppers and the sand on the seashore (see Judg. 7:12). Though they were clearly outnumbered, God still insisted Gideon's army was "too many" for Him to deliver the Midianites into their hands (see Judg. 7:2). They probably thought, *Too many, are you sure God?* The Lord knew what He was doing. He was going to defeat them supernaturally! In order to win in the battles of life and the things you feel are against you, you have to avoid excuses and distractions.

God tested the men's hearts to see who would be focused and put their hearts into obeying Him. This resulted in 22,000 of them leaving because they were afraid of the size of the opposing army. Now, this would leave just 10,000 in the army of Gideon remaining to fight! Even after this, God still wanted those who would be focused and have a different spirit, those who wouldn't be so easily distracted. He tested the men who remained by bringing them to the water. Why the water? It was for the purpose of self-examination, to see what was in their hearts and where their focus was. Would they trust God to defeat their enemy?

> *So Gideon took the men down to the water. There the LORD told him, "Separate those who lap the water with their tongues like a dog from those who kneel down to drink." Three hundred men lapped with their hands to their mouths. All the rest got down on their knees to drink. The LORD said to Gideon, "With the three hundred men that lapped I will save you and give the Midianites into your hands. Let all the other men go, each to his own place"* (Judges 7:5-7 NIV).

God brought a separation through the way they drank water. It sounds odd, doesn't it? What was God up to? God was revealing which soldiers were focused, committed, and fervent about their trust in Him. Any distractions, lack of focus, procrastination, or fear would have dangerous consequences. God needed those who would be focused.

This same principle will work in defeating Spiritual A.D.D. in your life today. What was the difference between the 9,700 who were drinking the water kneeling down and the 300 who drank the water lapping like a dog, cupping their hands and bringing it to their mouths? It was about the heart, and it revealed who was and who wasn't focused and committed. The ones who knelt down to drink had to put their faces in the water. This meant they would have to take their eyes off the enemy and become distracted by the blessing of the water.

Unfortunately, this is where many people live today. They take their eyes off God and even off the enemy to have a moment of drinking up all the blessings in life. Yes, they looked into the water, but it wasn't for self-examination but rather self-gratification, and they completely lost their focus and purpose. This is exactly how Spiritual A.D.D. works because it gets you off your focus and purpose by making other things look more gratifying, interesting, and appealing than spiritual things. As a result, you lose focus and fall prey to the enemy—not necessarily the devil, but the enemy of Spiritual A.D.D. Sadly, this is where some live; they base their spiritual lives solely on what is in it for them, on their needs and their feelings, and they completely lose sight of the spiritual tasks at hand.

The 300 who were chosen in Judges 7 lapped like a dog, putting their hands like cups up to their mouths to drink. This spoke of true focus and heart; they were able to enjoy blessings without losing focus or interest, especially on spiritual things. Remember, it would take a supernatural act of God to defeat a multitude of an army with only 300 men! They had a warrior mentality that kept their eyes on the enemy and that would forge through any challenge.

This is a beautiful picture of how we should handle things in this world. Sure, we can enjoy the rich blessings that this life provides, but we must not let the blessings put our spiritual lives and spiritual things out of focus! In the same way, we must keep our hearts in check and committed to God. This helps us overcome and not be hindered by the effects of Spiritual A.D.D.

Staying focused and committed while keeping your heart right and on God is important in your spiritual walk. It is so easy to get distracted, frustrated, or bored with the things of God if you are not wise. It comes down to spiritual focus, your heart, and your self-examination.

This same principle is also seen when God brought His people to the waters of self-examination in a place called the "waters of Marah" (see Exod. 15:23). Israel had just celebrated a major victory over Pharaoh and his army, and they even sang about God's great victory. However, there was a slight problem. This major victory was short-lived as it quickly turned into a session of complaining, murmuring, and lack of focus three days later. This happened because they had nothing to drink. The people complained that they were thirsty, and they began to take it out on Moses. So God made them "face themselves" by bringing them to the water for examination.

Why did God bring them to the waters of Marah? It was to show them their hearts and spiritual condition before the Lord. Just like with the brazen laver and the waters of Gideon, God wanted to show them that they were losing focus on Him and becoming distracted. Their hearts were wrong, and God wanted them to see it by a simple test of self-examination. He brought them to the water because it showed a reflection of their attitudes and their hearts.

Interestingly, the meaning of *Marah* in the Hebrew is "bitterness."[2] This was exactly how the Israelites were acting. Making them come, drink, and look into these bitter waters was God's way of giving an illustrated sermon—showing them their spiritual condition! He was making them face themselves.

As we can see in these examples, God used water for self-examination, and He still uses water today. You might be asking, "Water? What water is He using today?" It is the water of His Word, which is used for self-examination and focus. *"That He might sanctify and cleanse it with the washing of water by the word"* (Eph. 5:26). The Word of God is a measuring stick and standard by which you should live and gauge your spiritual progress.

The Bible mirrors or reflects your spiritual walk and how you are to conduct your life as a Christian. It is meant to keep you focused and to reveal your heart like the examples we read of the waters of examination.

Notice what the Book of James tells us about God's Word being a mirror, or reflection, of our spiritual condition.

> *But prove yourselves doers of the word, and not merely hearers who delude themselves. For if anyone is a hearer of the word and not a doer, he is like a man who looks at his natural face in a mirror; for once he has looked at himself and gone away, he has immediately forgotten what kind of person he was. But one who looks intently at the perfect law, the law of liberty, and abides by it, not having become a forgetful hearer but an effectual doer, this man will be blessed in what he does* (James 1:22-25 NASB).

We can see from these verses that there are two types of people. The first type is those who hear the Word and don't do it because they won't let the Word be the true reflection or standard by which they conduct their Christian walk. The second type is those who are faithful to hear the Word and do it because they have examined themselves, and they are blessed as a result.

This is often why people are distracted in regard to the Bible and seldom, if ever, read it. They don't want to have to face (like with the water) the things that are not right in their lives before the Lord. They don't want to be held accountable to what God has said in His Word. We must come to the Scriptures and adjust our lives to the standards that God has placed in His Word. It is not just enough to hear or read the Bible; we must do what it says.

People who don't want to be honest before God or themselves about their spiritual condition won't bother with self-examination and won't see God's Word as important for change. They will just be hearers only and not doers of the Word. This is often why some suffer in their spiritual lives.

It is important to know that the Word of God is for cleansing. It is perfect for cleansing your life and adjusting your walk and attitude. This is why the enemy loves, as the Scripture says, to steal the Word of God from people's hearts (see Mark 4:15), especially through the effects of Spiritual A.D.D. He knows that the Word of God is powerful and that it is your daily bread through which you grow spiritually. If he can convince you that the Word isn't working or is boring, if he can get you distracted from its importance, then he can frustrate your spiritual walk greatly.

The Bible is so powerful that it can be a mirror in your life and can be used for spiritual cleansing. The Word of God is used by the Holy Spirit as a mirror and a source of cleansing to convict and cause you to change your ways. This is what Jesus said in John chapter 15, *"Now ye are clean through the word which I have spoken unto you"* (John 15:3). This happens when you stay connected to the Lord through His Word and you start to bear fruit of Christian character.

When you examine yourself by the Word of God, you need to take what you read and apply it. The brazen laver did the priests no good unless they applied the water. In the same way, the Word isn't successful in overcoming Spiritual A.D.D. unless you apply it. It wasn't enough for them to just look at the laver and do nothing; neither is self-examination useful without action! Daily Bible reading and meditating, regardless of how you feel, is necessary for success against the symptoms of Spiritual A.D.D.

> *This book of the law shall not depart out of thy mouth; but thou shalt meditate therein day and night, that thou mayest observe to do according to all that is written therein: for then thou shalt make thy way prosperous, and then thou shalt have good success* (Joshua 1:8).

Go ahead, take that first step in overcoming Spiritual A.D.D., and pick up your Bible. Take a moment to pray and reflect, no matter how you feel or how bad things have become. I want to encourage you to take a moment of self-examination; do some soul searching, some inner reflecting on your spiritual walk, attitude, and pursuit. How are things really going? This isn't self–condemnation but rather self-examination. It is for the purpose of facing yourself so you can make the adjustments and changes necessary to defeat Spiritual A.D.D. in your life.

As you have you reflected for a moment and examined your life, you may have discovered that you are suffering from some of these symptoms and need to make some changes. If this is true, then you have passed the necessary part of the exam that starts with taking a self-exam. It is the start of a spiritual journey to the life and walk with God that you are crying out for. Continue to read and discover more truths to walking in a life of complete victory and satisfaction in Christ!

ENDNOTES

1. For more information, please see: www.symptomsadd.net; www.webmd.com/add-adhd/guide/adhd-symptoms; http://add.about.com/od/signsandsymptoms/a/symptoms.htm.

2. James Strong, *The New Strong's Exhaustive Concordance of the Bible* (Nashville, TN: Thomas Nelson, 1991), Hebrew #4785.

Chapter Two

I AM TIRED

And He cometh, and findeth them sleeping, and saith unto Peter, Simon, sleepest thou? couldest not thou watch one hour? (Mark 14:37)

"Hank, why don't you go rest a little and come back when we will both enjoy this?"

"What?" I said to myself. I was surprised by what I had heard in my heart, perceiving it was the voice of the Lord speaking to me. Yet, my rational, religious mind dismissed the gentle voice as just me making excuses so I could get out of praying.

SPIRITUAL A.D.D.

I had started earlier than usual that morning and was so excited to spend time with God, but I was falling asleep while praying. I would pray and then fall asleep, pray some more and then fall asleep again. I kept going in and out of sleep until, at one point, I caught myself praying about something ridiculous, mumbling as I continued in my devotions. I couldn't keep my eyes open and had exhausted every possible praying position I could imagine. I walked, knelt, stood, lay on my back, then lay face down. I even thought about praying standing on my head if it meant keeping me awake. (OK, not really, but you get the point.)

So, I decided, *I am going to just lie here before the Lord and pray.* Sure! You know what that means? I started fading fast, as my eyes got heavier and started nodding off to sleep. I often joke that Heaven started a countdown as they watched me fade into sleep mode. Ten, nine, eight, seven…. Yes, that's right, lights out! We all have had that moment of "lying" before the Lord only to awake from a brief "prayer nap."

This was exactly what was happening to me as I was trying to pray—until I heard what I believe was the Lord's voice interrupting me. I will never forget those words, "Hank, why don't you go rest and come back when we will both enjoy this?" Those words gave me a whole new perspective on how God views our time with Him. It also made me realize that I needed to try harder to value my moments with Him.

The Lord knew that I wasn't putting my heart into my prayer time and that deep inside of me I wanted to go back to bed. That's exactly what I did! I took God up on His suggestion and came back later to fellowship with Him when I was more rested. In this case, I found it easier to pray and comprehend what I was reading in Scripture after I had rested. Of course, it shouldn't be our norm to fall asleep and then come back later. We need to make sure we are getting plenty of rest so we can better focus on spiritual things and not fall asleep.

Maybe you are falling asleep regularly in prayer and devotions. Perhaps you are bored with spiritual things. What do you do if it is common for you to fall asleep or feel worn out in your spiritual walk, especially if you are getting plenty of rest? In this chapter, I will give some pointers that may be a help and encouragement as you are deciding if "waking up" is something that needs to be addressed in your life.

It Is Time to Wake Up

You might be saying, "But, I am tired! You don't know my situation." I do understand, and I have felt that way too—to the point of falling asleep in my prayer time, as I mentioned before. Consistently falling asleep in prayer and Bible devotions could be a sign of Spiritual A.D.D.; the good news is, there is hope and an answer.

SPIRITUAL A.D.D.

First you have to recognize the danger of falling asleep, spiritual slumber, and stupor before I address the solution. It can be very frustrating or discouraging to your spiritual walk, often leaving you with a feeling of emptiness with God and little to no results in prayer. When this is the outcome time and time again, it is easy to become bored with spiritual things. You can become bored with prayer or reading the Bible, feel church isn't important anymore, and believe that trying to seek God is a real chore! This is because spiritual boredom, which is one of the symptoms of Spiritual A.D.D., has set in. This leads to tiredness and eventual slumber, with the constant struggle to stay interested in spiritual things.

This happened with Jesus' disciples when He asked them to pray with Him at a time when He really wanted their support in prayer. After all, that's why He had brought them. *"And He cometh, and findeth them sleeping, and saith unto Peter, Simon, sleepest thou? couldest not thou watch one hour?"* (Mark 14:37). Jesus was telling them to wake up because they had fallen asleep in prayer.

Falling asleep and tiredness kept the disciples from being able to pray for an hour. I always make it my goal to pray at least an hour during my devotional time. This is especially important for those who have been Christians for a while. The disciples had been with Jesus three years, and He expected them to be able to pray at least an hour.

Pray for an entire hour? Are you serious? Yes, I am! You can pray for an hour, especially if you have been serving the Lord awhile. It isn't that difficult. If you are going to get serious about overcoming Spiritual A.D.D., you need to be able to pray longer, stronger, and more consistently. This is what you need to do if you really want results and a satisfying spiritual walk.

You may be asking, "Where is the first place to start in the path to freedom from Spiritual A.D.D.?" The first place to start is always with the heart attitude. Without it you will just spin your spiritual wheels and become frustrated. If you go into your time with God acting like it is boring and inconvenient, it will affect your time with Him. I try to approach my time with God with excitement, joy, and expectation. Get excited about the time that you will be with Him, rather than dragging yourself to be in His presence.

Once you submit your heart and develop the right attitude of joy and excitement, the next step is to establish a time when you will meet with Him (this needs to be consistent). Plan your time and place to meet with the Lord. For those struggling with Spiritual A.D.D., I suggest planning out a one-hour time frame. That gives you plenty of time to worship God, talk with Him, pray, and read your Bible.

I have also found it beneficial to have things I want to discuss with Him written down. Making a list of things you want to talk to God about will keep you on track and focused, helping you to make better use of your time with Him. It will help you accomplish the things you desire while not feeling like you're just shooting in the dark with your prayers.

Another helpful thing I have found in my devotional time is to try not to approach it as an hour of just me talking. I mix it up with worship, Bible reading, prayer, asking God questions, and waiting for Him to answer. Sometimes I just rest before the Lord in His presence, letting Him minister to me.

These are merely suggestions to get you on track. The important thing is a regular and consistent time that is enjoyable and gets results. The key is to be well-organized and disciplined, yet not rigid and uptight, because that will take the joy out of your relationship with Him.

Here is a format you can consider which will help you have more effective times with God for at least an hour! It is a simple (though certainly not required) example of how to use an hour to your benefit and the Lord's. Remember my story? God wanted me to come back when my heart was in it and more rested. Always remember, prayer is a relationship. It's not just a one-sided discussion but rather a conversation with God! The more real you will make God in your life, the more real He will become to you, thus helping you to kick Spiritual

A.D.D. out of your life. Try out this list for a while until you establish—or reestablish—one that works for you!

Activation

The purpose of this activation is to help people to start, get back to, or further develop 30 minutes to one hour of daily private prayer. The five minutes on each of the suggestions below is for a 30-minute plan, and the ten minutes is for a one-hour plan. These are simply suggestions. The key is doing what works for you and stretches you. Start small and increase!

Set a Time

The first thing to do is establish a meeting time. The best time is always first thing in your day. Keep your time realistic and consistent to what works for your schedule. Avoid extreme times and lengths when you first start, which will only lead to discouragement and the desire to quit. If you are falling asleep in prayer, an evening routine may work for a season until you build consistency to return to a morning routine instead.

Set a Place

After you set a meeting time that works and is realistic, you need to establish a meeting place that gives you that "private room" that Jesus mentioned in Matthew 6:6. You can change this depending on space and location. The key is to keep it fun and exciting—a place you enjoy being that is void of distractions.

Worship and Search Your Heart

(5 or 10 minutes) Begin your prayer time by fellowshipping with the Father. Sing songs to Him, talk to Him, and spend time getting to know Him. Worship Him, declaring His greatness. This is also a great time to search your heart and confess your sins, receiving His forgiveness.

Give a Moment of Thanks

(5 or 10 minutes) This is time when you thank God for who He is and what He has done. It is important to be specific and grateful when it comes to God's blessings and provisions.

Pray in the Spirit or Ask God Questions, Listening to Him

(5 or 10 minutes) Pray in the Spirit. Pray with fervency of spirit, soul, and body. Let the Holy Spirit pray through you as you yield to the different diversities and utterances as you pray in the Spirit. Set a timer if you have to, as you build intensity in the spirit realm. Or you can use this time to wait on the Lord to speak and minister to you.

Declare His Word and Pray the Word

(5 or 10 minutes) Take a moment to declare His Word in your life and over your loved ones. Pray Scriptures

you have memorized, or pray God's Word from the Bible. Remember, God listens for and listens to His Word when it is spoken.

Make Your Requests Known

(5 or 10 minutes) It is important to come into God's throne room prepared. He said to make your requests known to Him. *"Be careful for nothing; but in every thing by prayer and supplication with thanksgiving let your requests be made known unto God"* (Phil. 4:6). A helpful tool is a notebook and writing instrument. I recommend writing down your list of prayer requests and leaving space where you can write things that you may hear, sense, or see in prayer.

Pray for Others

(5 or 10 minutes) Make a list of names and prayer requests for others. Take a little time to pray over and intercede for those on your list. Having a list to pray about for yourself and for others is a great way for you see God's answers to prayer. It will help you to offer thanks to God for answered prayer and also to build your faith.

I pray that as you read through this list of activation steps, you will begin to have renewed hope that you can do it. This pattern may be helpful as is, or perhaps you will adjust the list to make one of your own. Just remember that your spiritual walk and time with God is only good to the proportion that you are willing to invest in it. It requires your heart, time, focus, diligence, sacrifice, and commitment. When you commit to these things, Spiritual A.D.D. won't take root in your life.

Others Who Slept

Sometimes, no matter how good the plan is, it can still be easy to suffer from Spiritual A.D.D. and resort to quitting because you keep falling asleep or you feel spiritually exhausted. This scenario often leaves people asking, "Why try?" Those who have Spiritual A.D.D. often fall asleep in God's presence and, as a result, feel guilty. *"Slothfulness casteth into a deep sleep; and an idle soul shall suffer hunger"* (Prov. 19:15).

Sometimes you may fall asleep or experience spiritual apathy because of a lack of rest, which makes you tired. One of the greatest enemies to the power of God in people's lives is lack of rest. God rested on the last day of creation and established a day of rest thereafter (see Gen. 2:2; Exod. 31:17; Heb. 4:9-11). *"The Sabbath was made for man, and not man for the Sabbath"* (Mark 2:27).

It is vital to get a good night's rest so it will be easier to pray without falling asleep. Typically, I have found it more difficult to stay focused in spiritual things when I am tired. As I have mentioned, occasionally I have times in my devotions when I will allow myself to fall into a short sleep, resting before the Lord. Sometimes it is OK to fall asleep while studying the Word or praying; then after your short nap, you can return to your devotions with God. However, this can become a habitual condition of falling asleep or spiritual apathy if you allow it too often or if you just throw your hands in the air in frustration. If this is a normal pattern, you are probably suffering from Spiritual A.D.D., which needs to be addressed if you want to enjoy a spiritual life that is productive

If this is true of you, the important thing is to not feel guilty and condemn yourself. Realize that if people were more honest, more of them would admit they have Spiritual A.D.D. too. In fact, many people have fallen asleep at some time in their devotional time. When we look at the Scriptures, we see some who did as well. The Bible tells us not to fall asleep as others do, but to stay alert. *"Therefore let us not sleep, as do others; but let us watch and be sober"* (1 Thess. 5:6). Let's look at some examples from the Bible and see how they can prophetically apply to us today. As we look at each one, we can also gain insight on how to defeat this symptom of Spiritual A.D.D. in our lives.

The Sleep of Jacob—Genesis 28

Jacob fell asleep and didn't realize that God had visited Him while he was sleeping. He also realized that there is a heavenly ladder (access) available for those who will stay awake and take advantage of the covenant right to heavenly blessings and answers. Some people today, because of Spiritual A.D.D., are in the "sleep of Jacob"—they struggle to receive answers to prayers and their heavenly benefits, and they don't experience the presence of God because they are asleep. It's important to stay awake and spiritually alert. When we pray, God is listening or speaking to us, but we will miss it if we are in a state of spiritual stupor and tiredness like Jacob was. *"When Jacob awoke from his sleep, he thought, 'Surely the Lord is in this place, and I was not aware of it'"* (Gen. 28:16 NIV).

The Sleep of Samson—Judges 16

When Samson was lulled to sleep by Delilah, he was seduced into revealing the source of his strength, his obedience to God by not cutting his hair. This type of sleep is dangerous to those who won't address Spiritual A.D.D. and their struggles with falling asleep or being lulled to sleep by the enemy. This is because, like Samson, they awake presuming they have the strength to defeat the enemy. But they struggle to do so because they are too spiritually weak and have been seduced into a life of spiritual compromise by the enemy. As a result, their prayer lives start weakening more and more over time until they want to give up. According to Jesus, prayer is what makes us strong and keeps us from fainting. *"And He spake a parable unto them to this end, that men ought always to pray, and not to faint"* (Luke 18:1).

The Sleep of Jonah—Jonah 1

Jonah was told by the Lord to go and prophesy to the city of Nineveh to repent. But he refused and instead ran from the Lord, falling asleep on a ship taking him in the opposite direction from where God wanted him to go. This kind of sleep symptom arises in Spiritual A.D.D. when people are not submitted to the will of God; such sleep can cause them to spiritually drift like Jonah in the boat. This is where spiritual slumber can lead to disobedience and a hardening of the heart toward God's will, which eventually causes them to run away from spiritual things because they are drifting in spiritual apathy.

The Sleep of Eli the Priest—First Samuel 3

Eli the priest became a heavy man whose eyes became dim, and he was unable to discern the voice of the Lord speaking to his young protégé, Samuel. The reason for Eli's condition, according to the Bible, was that he lay down to rest in his own place while Samuel rested where the presence of God was (see 1 Sam. 3:2-3). Failure to address this spiritual sleep condition and the symptoms of Spiritual A.D.D. may cause people, like Eli, to become spiritually weighed down, their spiritual eyes becoming dim. It becomes harder for them to hear the voice of the Lord and His direction for their lives. The key is to rest in the presence of God, not falling asleep, but spending time in His presence like Samuel did.

The Sleep of Uriah—Second Samuel 11

King David had committed adultery with Bathsheba, the wife of one of his key warriors. In order to cover it up, David suggested that this warrior, Uriah, go from the battle he was fighting for David to his own house to be with his wife, Bathsheba. But Uriah, a faithful and loyal soldier, decided that instead of going home to be with his wife he would stay close to his job and his boss, King David. He elected to sleep outside the doors of the palace, working overtime and neglecting his home due to his loyalty to his boss and job.

This may sound crazy, but it is often why some suffer with Spiritual A.D.D. They are more loyal, faithful, and dedicated to their boss and employment than to their time with God. If people choose to prioritize God and His Kingdom as first, making Him the highest thing on their daily agendas, their homes and spiritual lives won't suffer as much. Dedication, commitment, and fervor in employment are important, but not at the expense of falling asleep, thus damaging fellowship with God and causing homes to suffer because priorities are out of order.

Sitting Too Close to the Edge

Here is yet another biblical example of a person who fell asleep, in addition to the ones we have just read.

As we look at this story, we will find it isn't just about falling asleep. It also prophetically represents a spiritual state that affects some individuals and some churches. We can learn a lot from the example that we find in Acts chapter 20—the story of a young man named Eutychus who fell asleep.

> *We met on Sunday to worship and celebrate the Master's Supper. Paul addressed the congregation. Our plan was to leave first thing in the morning, but Paul talked on, way past midnight. We were meeting in a well-lighted upper room. A young man named Eutychus was sitting in an open window. As Paul went on and on, Eutychus fell sound asleep and toppled out the third-story window. When they picked him up, he was dead* (Acts 20:7-9 MSG).

Imagine, right in the middle of the sermon, someone falls out a window three stories high to his death! This is no laughing matter. Yet, in this story, we discover that the apostle Paul was preaching until midnight in a place called an upper chamber. My wife and I often tease each other with this example of Paul being long-winded. We have all probably known a long-winded preacher or sat through a long sermon somewhere. My wife and I always joke about which one of us is the longer-winded preacher. Of course, I say it's her, and she says it's me, but neither of us has ever preached until midnight like Paul. But we have had some fall asleep while we preached!

SPIRITUAL A.D.D.

Eutychus fell asleep during Paul's sermon while he was listening in a window. Probably it wasn't a good place to be sitting since he was tired. This story reveals some truths of how Spiritual A.D.D. is affecting some people in their individual lives and others while in the church. It could be said that Eutychus was sitting in a place that can cause Spiritual A.D.D.—living too close to the edge. He fell three stories to his death and had to be brought back to life by Paul!

It is safe to assume that Eutychus was sitting facing Paul, with his back toward the outside. This means he fell backward! Often we talk about people who are *backsliding*—people who are not walking with the Lord as they should or who have fallen into a state of apathy and are not pressing in and really serving the Lord. This can happen if they are sitting too close to the edge in their lives like Eutychus did in the window. When Spiritual A.D.D. starts affecting people, some choose to sit too close to things in this life that may cause them to fall backward and away from God. For some, it is immediate, and for others, it happens over a time of constant falling asleep or through an attitude of apathy that causes them to drift closer to the edge. They sit there in this state until, like Eutychus, they fall from a high place in their spiritual walk, and then they need to be resuscitated.

This is why we have to take a serious and hard look at our spiritual condition. Are we allowing the symptoms of Spiritual A.D.D. to cause us to sit too close to the edge? We know we are being affected when we are falling asleep spiritually and becoming dull of hearing. We begin to lose interest in spiritual things because we are spiritually sleepy, disinterested, or distracted. All of this happens because we are trying to see how close we can live to the edge of spiritual compromise without falling. This is why we have to address Spiritual A.D.D.; it can lead to us falling away from God, to backsliding.

We must avoid this spiritual state or spiritual stupor. Look at the definitions in the Greek for the word *sleeping* that was used to describe Eutychus. The word *sleeping* is the Greek word *hupros*. This word means to sleep or a figuratively spiritual torpor or sleep.[1] Now, the word *torpor*, which is used to describe the kind of sleep Eutychus fell into, means a state of being dormant or inactive; a temporary loss of all or part of the power of sensation or motion: sluggishness, stupor, dullness, apathy. It is a state of mental or physical inactivity or instability, lethargy, and apathy. It also means dormant or an inactive state of hibernating. Wow! It's sobering to look at these definitions describing what kind of sleep he fell into.

This shows that falling into this spiritual state is serious and must be avoided! From these definitions, we can also see the importance of resisting this spiritual slumber and state if we want to have a successful spiritual walk. They also reveal how detrimental to our lives a constant habit of falling asleep or a constant state of spiritual apathy can be. This is why we need to address this symptom of Spiritual A.D.D. and drive it from our lives.

Jesus understood this danger. He further illustrated it and the consequences for those who fall asleep in spiritual things or live in spiritual apathy in Matthew chapter 13. He revealed that, if we don't address the enemy who comes while we are sleeping to take the Word sown into our hearts, the enemy will sow tares in our lives, which can affect the will of God concerning us. These tares the devil sows can be distractions, sins, or other things that seek to destroy our spiritual lives. The importance of resisting Spiritual A.D.D. is obvious. The enemy tries to attack when we are asleep. *"But while men slept, his enemy came and sowed tares among the wheat, and went his way"* (Matt. 13:25).

You must ask yourself some important questions. Are you falling asleep in spiritual things? Has spiritual apathy for the things of God caused you to start spiritually drifting? Is your attitude toward your spiritual life, "Whatever will be, will be"? If this is the case, you may be experiencing the effects of Spiritual A.D.D. It is important to rise up and shake it off!

It's Time to Shake It Off

I am not talking about a wild new dance craze, but of a spiritual action that affects your spirit, soul, and body. The Scriptures tell us to shake ourselves. *"Shake thyself from the dust; arise, and sit down, O Jerusalem: loose thyself from the bands of thy neck, O captive daughter of Zion"* (Isa. 52:2).

Shake off the dust! You know that dusty Bible that hasn't been read in a while. How about that dusty lack of commitment to finding, joining, and getting involved in a good church? What about shaking off the dust of earthly things that are weighing you down, causing you to sin and fall into spiritual apathy? Whatever the dust is that has been allowed in your life, it needs to be shaken from you!

We need to do what this verse says and shake such things from us, loosing ourselves from the things that are trying to cause tiredness, boredom, and spiritual apathy. How do we do that? Sometimes we have to literally shake ourselves to keep from falling asleep or becoming lethargic in spiritual things. This can happen in prayer, and it is referred to as spiritual heaviness: *"… the garment of praise for the spirit of heaviness…"* (Isa. 61:3).

This heaviness, which comes when we are spending time in spiritual things or is an aspect of our spiritual condition, can be an evil spirit of heaviness. This spirit, as Jesus mentioned, wants to sow tares into our lives and does so through a heaviness often found in Spiritual A.D.D. One of the ways to defeat this spirit of heaviness is by praising and worshipping God. A life of worship helps to strengthen us, as well as causing spiritual resistance from the enemy to go.

We find an example of this with King Saul. When he was tired and under attack from the enemy, only worship and praise that David gave to the Lord in King Saul's presence refreshed him and made the evil spirit leave.

> *And whenever the tormenting spirit from God troubled Saul, David would play the harp. Then Saul would feel better, and the tormenting spirit would go away* (1 Samuel 16:23 NLT).

I encourage you to put on some Christian praise music and begin worshipping the Lord. Don't be afraid to address that spirit of heaviness and tell it to leave your life!

At other times, you may need to take a moment to shake yourself (of course, not to hurt yourself). I know this may sound silly. Please don't misunderstand me, but sometimes, in my own time of prayer, I have had to literally shake my hands, shake my head, and jump up and down to wake up. Something else I do is to take a few minutes standing in place and begin worshipping God or praying in the spirit as strong as I can with all my body, soul, and spirit. I am not talking about waking up the neighbors and scaring the cat, but I am talking about a fervency and determination to stir up my spirit and cause my body and soul to do so as well. This is what the apostle Paul referred to when he mentioned what he does to shake himself up.

> *Therefore I do not run like a man running aimlessly; I do not fight like a man beating the air. No, I beat my body and make it my slave so that after I have preached to others, I myself will not be disqualified for the prize* (1 Corinthians 9:26-27 NIV).

This is a process that Paul is speaking about, and it doesn't require physical torture! Instead you can do this method of shaking yourself up by walking, pacing, standing, and shaking yourself. It's not so much a physical shaking as a determination to stir yourself up to break Spiritual A.D.D. from causing a spiritual sleep. The Message translation of Scripture says that Paul shakes himself up to keep himself from being caught napping! *"...I'm not going to get caught napping, telling everyone else all about it and then missing out myself"* (1 Cor. 9:27 MSG). Shaking yourself is a self-discipline and determination to resist things that are trying to steal from your spiritual walk. It is praying earnestly and pressing into what you are praying, worshipping, or doing for the Lord. This keeps you from falling asleep.

SPIRITUAL A.D.D.

It's kind of like runners before race: They take a few moments to shake themselves by moving their heads, hands, and bodies. This keeps them loose and helps them to focus. *"I discipline my body like an athlete, training it to do what it should"* (1 Cor. 9:27 NLT).

If you are struggling, why not just begin to worship God? Try pressing into Him, no matter how you sound or feel at that moment. The results will be the same as what happened for King Saul. It will refresh you, causing the enemy to leave, and it will lift that heaviness and burden from you!

One key difference I want to point out between David, who wasn't affected by an evil spirit, and Saul, who was oppressed, is that David didn't need anything or anyone to be his spiritual cheerleader or worship leader. It's not wrong to need that, but true spiritual strength comes when you learn to develop it on your own. David was able to do this himself by pressing into God when he was alone, unlike King Saul, who needed someone else to help him worship, praise, experience God, and get a spiritual breakthrough.

As I said before, sometimes Spiritual A.D.D. can come from the devil, also known as the spirit of heaviness. We need to shake it off. This is what happened to Paul in Acts 28 when he was bit by a snake that fastened to his hand.

And when Paul had gathered a bundle of sticks, and laid them on the fire, there came a viper out of the heat, and fastened on his hand (Acts 28:3).

Those standing by were watching as he was bit, and they expected him to fall over dead. Paul didn't die, nor was he affected by this snakebite. Instead Paul's answer was to shake it off and continue on without the effects of the enemy. He just shook off that viper attack! *"And he shook off the beast into the fire, and felt no harm"* (Acts 28:5). This is exactly what we need to do with Spiritual A.D.D.—heaviness, lethargy, tiredness, and all other symptoms. I encourage you to make that choice and shake it off, loosing yourself from captivity!

Are you ready to shake it off? Here are some things you can consider to prevent you from falling asleep in prayer or into a spiritual state of apathy:

1. *Get plenty of rest*—Try to maintain a normal sleep schedule and routine, if possible. Failure to do so is one of the biggest reasons people suffer with Spiritual A.D.D., and it keeps them from being focused in their times with God.

2. *Take a moment to wake up*—Take a shower, wash your face, watch the weather forecast, drink a hot cup of coffee, or do some other arousing activity. This is helpful to some,

rather than diving head-first into their time with God if they are tired. A brief moment to wake up may help you more than you realize. My wife, Brenda, jokes that she can't talk to anyone when she first wakes up, even God. She likes a fresh cup of coffee to start her day first.

3. *Have your devotions in a well-lit place*—Once in prayer, keep the lights on, as it is easier to fall asleep when it's dark. Changing your prayer location and routine maybe be helpful and give you a needed spark of encouragement as well.

4. *Have a little praise music or background noise*—It is helpful to have some faint noise, which will help you to stay awake, yet not become distracted.

5. *Try new prayer positions*—Try positions that promote staying awake, like walking and pacing. It is probably not wise to try to pray while you are in bed and comfortable. Again, try not to "lie before the Lord" in prayer at first. Get out of bed and start off by walking, pacing, kneeling, or sitting with plenty of light to keep you alert.

6. *Pray the Word of God out loud*—Select Scriptures that go with your situation. This is also a type of praying with Jesus, praying His Word.

7. *Get a prayer partner to help you in your prayer life*—This is what Jesus tried to accomplish in the Garden of Gethsemane. "Could you not pray with Me?" Jesus said this to the disciples (see Mark 14:37). Pray with a friend, either on the telephone or in person. It is a great way to keep you awake and hold yourself and another person accountable to pray.

Now that you have either tried or are considering some of these things, you are ready to rise up and defeat Spiritual A.D.D. in your life, especially spiritual fatigue!

Stir Yourself Up

If we are going to shake off and defeat Spiritual A.D.D. in our lives, it will require spiritual determination. David modeled such determination in Psalm 132.

Surely I will not come into the tabernacle of my house, nor go up into my bed; I will not give sleep to mine eyes, or slumber to mine eyelids, until I find out a place for the LORD, an habitation for the mighty God of Jacob (Psalm 132:3-5).

SPIRITUAL A.D.D.

David was determined that nothing would stop him from being in the presence of God. He stirred himself up, saying that he wouldn't slumber or sleep until he found a place for the Lord. He definitely wasn't going to stay in spiritual neutral; he was in high gear in his pursuit of the Lord. This is the same kind of determination that we need to stir ourselves up in the things of the Lord.

This kind of determination is a great way to defeat Spiritual A.D.D., tiredness, and spiritual apathy. It requires learning how to shift gears from a life in neutral to a life running in a higher gear of spiritual fervency and pursuit. It is called stirring yourself up. It keeps you from remaining in neutral, not going anywhere or accomplishing what you want for the Lord. This shifting of gears comes through the decision to stir yourself up, regardless of how you feel.

Stirring yourself up and shifting spiritual gears is like learning to drive a car with a stick and clutch. In order to reach your desired destination, you can't stay in neutral, and you need to know how to shift the gears at the proper time. It is also important, if you want to go faster and farther, to know how to shift into a higher gear when needed.

When I first learned to drive a standard transmission, which requires manually shifting gears, it was no easy task for me, as I am not always the most coordinated person. It was a real challenge. In fact, my wife, Brenda, had to teach me. We were engaged at the time, and she had her hands full trying to teach me, especially since I can be determined in my own ways. I wasn't doing well learning on her car, and I even ruined the radiator by overheating it. It wasn't long after this that she finally asked her dad to teach me instead. That was over 20 years ago, and I am happy to say that I know how to drive a stick with ease today. In fact, I love driving antique cars that have standard transmissions and require me to shift from gear to gear.

The point of this story is that it took me some time, at first, to learn how to shift from neutral to first and then go from gear to gear without jerking, stalling, and damaging the car. The same is true in the spirit and in attempts to overcome Spiritual A.D.D. You might jerk, overheat, stall, and feel like quitting—all the same things that may happen to a person learning to drive stick. The moment you decide to get it into gear and really prioritize the Lord, prayer, Bible reading, going to church, and your spiritual life in general, you may feel like you're learning to drive stick in the spirit.

"Stick" with it; you will be glad you did! If you will stick with it, the Lord will help you shift from neutral into gear until you are running smoothly on all spiritual cylinders. He is also excellent at teaching you when to slow down and when to speed up. He knows how to teach you to not grind your spiritual gears in frustration, causing damage to your spiritual life.

How do you apply this to your life, and just how do you shift into gear from a life of Spiritual A.D.D.? You have to stir yourself up! That is how you shift spiritual gears. This is exactly what the apostle Paul told his young protégé, Timothy—to stir himself up, especially in the gifts of God.

> *Wherefore I put thee in remembrance that thou stir up the gift of God, which is in thee by the putting on of my hands* (2 Timothy 1:6).

We have to stir ourselves up! The responsibility is on us to stir ourselves up, and there are many ways to do it. It starts with a return to spiritual fervency, which gives a powerful victory against Spiritual A.D.D.! We are told in Scripture that we need to live our Christian lives in spiritual fervency. *"Never be lacking in zeal, but keep your spiritual fervor, serving the Lord"* (Rom. 12:11 NIV). This means we have to press in with fervency if we want spiritual victory and success.

In order to do this, stir yourself up by trying to put more heart, emotion, and spirit into your prayers and overall Christian attitude. God is waiting and expecting you to shift gears and stir yourself up, avoiding spiritual sleep and slumber. *"And there is none that calleth upon Thy name, that stirreth up himself to take hold of Thee…"* (Isa. 64:7).

When we press into God with a determination and excitement about spiritual things, it stirs us up and brings proper balance to our lives. When making Kool-Aid, if we add the Kool-Aid packet and a whole bunch of sugar to the water, but don't stir it, the contents will fall to the bottom and it won't taste very good. In the same way, spiritually speaking, God has given us all the ingredients we need to enjoy life, especially with Him. However, if we don't press in and pursue Him, no matter what great things He has provided for us, we will start to settle down in our lives. Then, like with the Kool-Aid, we get out of balance and experience a separation—until we stir ourselves back up. Once we stir the Kool-Aid, it tastes better, looks better, and can be enjoyed.

Take a few minutes to stir your heart up; focus on the Lord and pick up that Bible again. When you do, you are stirring yourself up and beginning the necessary process to build a spiritual life that is well balanced and through which you will receive the maximum benefits. Start shifting and you will make it to your finish line!

ENDNOTE

1. James Strong, *The New Strong's Exhaustive Concordance of the Bible* (Nashville, TN: Thomas Nelson, 1991), Greek #5258.

Chapter Three

WINNING THE RACE OF THE MIND

In your patience possess ye your souls (Luke 21:19).

"Whoa!! Whoa!" I kept repeating, but to no avail. I had agreed to go horseback riding with some of my friends. But the horse that I was riding took off running wildly with me holding the reins loosely and screaming for this seemingly "demonic" horse to stop. The more I yelled, the faster he seemed to go; at one point he even ran under a tree as if to try to knock me off. I finally let go of the reins and held on to the saddle. I hadn't really ridden a horse before and was getting a very fast lesson. It seemed this crazy animal was enjoying every moment of it, knowing I was a scared new rider. I kept yelling, hoping the horse would slow down, all the while not realizing that the ability to control this horse was right in my hands. I had the reins to help determine his direction, to slow him down, and to make him stop—the power was right in my hands! The problem was I was holding them too loosely, and then I let go of them. Eventually one of my friends, who was an experienced rider, grabbed the reins of the horse I was riding and made him come to a stop.

This is often how we deal with the Spiritual A.D.D. trying to attack our lives. We tend to let our minds and our schedules take off wildly, and we just go along for the ride. We often go through life and spiritual moments with God that are running out of our control, like the horse I was riding. It is hard for us to focus, pray, and get excited about spiritual things, so we just keep letting our minds wander. And we do nothing about our out-of-control schedules, which keep us from a consistent life with God.

We have a God who is with us along the journey. But the Lord has put the decision and power in our hands (just like I had the reins for the horse I was riding). We are able to address our minds when they wander in prayer. We can create a solution for the continual distractions and the out-of-control schedules, which are not only symptoms of Spiritual A.D.D but are hindrances to a spiritually satisfied life.

Go Ahead, Pull the Reins

We have to pull the reins and say to our minds and any symptoms of Spiritual A.D.D., "Whoa, you aren't going to wander and get out of control!" This is also what Jesus meant by "possessing our souls" (see Luke 21:19). Our souls are made up of our minds, our wills, and our emotions. They are like the horse I was riding, always trying to run wild. We have to pull back on the reins and slow the horse down. The same is true with our minds when they try to pull us away from spiritual things. We must respond immediately by taking the reins, gaining control, slowing down, and bringing our minds and thoughts in order by determining that we are going to focus on and pursue God.

We are spirits, we have souls (minds, wills, and emotions), and we live in physical bodies.

> *And the very God of peace sanctify you wholly; and I pray God your whole spirit and soul and body be preserved blameless unto the coming of our Lord Jesus Christ* (1 Thessalonians 5:23).

We are triune beings created by God Himself. Whenever we have thoughts that distract us from the things of God, it is helpful to immediately address those thoughts by speaking to them. Tell yourself that you are going to have a successful, fruitful time with the Lord; all other thoughts are to be taken captive to the obedience of Christ.

> *(For the weapons of our warfare are not carnal, but mighty through God to the pulling down of strong holds;) casting down imaginations, and every high thing that exalteth itself against the knowledge of God, and bringing into captivity every thought to the obedience of Christ* (2 Corinthians 10:4-5).

This is what we are referring to as "pulling on the reins"—we address Spiritual A.D.D. and take our thoughts captive to the obedience of Christ. When you pull the reins during your time with God, you tell your mind to be quiet with a determination that you are going to pray, read your Bible, and press into spiritual things. It is about making righteous and godly decisions and holding on tightly to your spiritual time and your desire to seek the things of God.

Notice what Jesus did with the fig tree when He noticed it didn't have any fruit on it.

> *And seeing a fig tree afar off having leaves, He came, if haply He might find any thing thereon: and when He came to it, He found nothing but leaves; for the time of figs was not yet. And Jesus answered and said unto it, No man eat fruit of thee hereafter for ever. And His disciples heard it* (Mark 11:13-14).

Perhaps Jesus immediately addressed this fig tree in response to thoughts the enemy may have been trying to attack Him with, suggesting that His ministry was fruitless like this fig tree. However, He did not listen to these thoughts, but He spoke and took His thoughts captive to the purposes of His Father.

We can learn from this example what we need to do when something is trying to interrupt our spiritual walk and the spiritual things we want to do for and with the Lord. We need to speak to it and address it. This is vital because, if these things are not immediately dealt with, they will become stronger and we will lose the battle, eventually giving in to Spiritual A.D.D. Over time, if we are not careful, we may begin to accept things as they are. These hindrances can even affect our feelings of self-worth, causing us to feel like failures, spiritually inadequate, and to condemn ourselves before the Lord.

How we see ourselves often determines our success. *"For as he thinketh in his heart, so is he…"* (Prov. 23:7). If we see ourselves as people who can't focus on God, who are always distracted in spiritual things, and who constantly suffer from Spiritual A.D.D., then we probably will end up becoming exactly that. If we think of ourselves as spiritual failures who will never be able to enjoy the benefits of seeking God, then we most likely will become just that.

SPIRITUAL A.D.D.

This is why many quit in their pursuit of God and have decided, "Why bother?" Their self-worth has been redefined by their constant struggles. Instead, we must speak to ourselves. We all talk to ourselves at times. In fact, the Bible even tells us to. *"Speaking to yourselves in psalms and hymns and spiritual songs, singing and making melody in your heart to the Lord"* (Eph. 5:19).

Sometimes you have to look at yourself in the mirror and speak to yourself! You have to tell your body to wake up and your mind to quit wandering. Eye-to-eye contact with yourself may be difficult, but it's necessary. In fact, most of what you hear and say comes from yourself. No one forms your outlook, mindset, and decisions more than you. This is why speaking to yourself to address the things that are trying to interrupt your spiritual life and time is so important. It is another way of possessing your soul. You have to address yourself and your situation so that you can experience a positive outcome.

This is exactly what King David did. He spoke to himself, and he spoke to his soul. He commanded his soul to wake up and bless the Lord.

> *Bless the Lord, O my soul: and all that is within me, bless His holy name. Bless the Lord, O my soul, and forget not all His benefits* (Psalm 103:1-2).

David was speaking to his soul, which is the mind, will, and emotions. He told his soul to bless the Lord.

Don't let your soul tell you what you are going to do or what your attitude is. You have to address your soul and speak to yourself. In fact, this verse denotes that it is a choice to keep your soul in line. The Hebrew word for *bless* in this verse is *barak*, and it means to bow or kneel as in prayer, worship, or praise.[1] David was saying to himself, "I will bless the Lord, and I will do it by bowing with my whole heart. I am telling my soul what to do, not my soul telling me. I am not going to let it steal my time with God."

Do you see it? He was pulling the reins on his soul! This same action will work for you and will help you greatly in overcoming Spiritual A.D.D. The more you pull the reins by addressing and speaking to things that want to cause disruptions and make your mind wander in spiritual things, the more you will win the spiritual tug-of-war, so to speak, between your soul, flesh, and spirit.

Win the Tug-of-War

The trinity of God is the Father, Son, and Holy Ghost; the trinity of humanity is spirit, soul, and body. Your spirit is stronger and more dominant than your body or soul because the spirit is created in the image of God. This is why it can often be a struggle to keep your soul and body involved in your spiritual pursuit. God is a spirit, and the way to connect with Him is from your spirit to His spirit—with your soul and body coming in line with your spiritual pursuit. Jesus even mentioned this when explaining how to worship God. *"God is a Spirit: and they that worship Him must worship Him in spirit and in truth"* (John 4:24).

When you rise up in your spirit by stirring yourself up and speaking to yourself, your spirit gets stronger, and your body and soul will follow, resulting in the defeat of Spiritual A.D.D. in your life! The power to pray and win this tug-of-war between the spirit and the body and soul comes as you rise up in your spirit. Jesus too had to rise up in His spirit. He did this when He was in the Garden of Gethsemane with His disciples.

> *And He taketh with Him Peter and James and John, and began to be sore amazed, and to be very heavy [He was feeling the pressure of the death He was about to face—there was so much pressure coming at Him in His soul]; and saith unto them, My soul is exceeding sorrowful unto death: tarry ye here, and watch. And He went forward a little, and fell on the ground, and prayed that, if it were possible, the hour might pass from Him* (Mark 14:33-35).

Jesus faced so much pressure that the Bible says He sweated great drops of blood (see Luke 22:44). He had to rise up in His spirit, or all hope would have been lost! You can imagine the pressure because the purpose for His life and all humankind would be lost if He failed to rise up in His spirit, submitting His body and soul when He prayed. He had to stay in a spiritual mindset and even resist being distracted by His disciples, who slept even though three times He asked for their help in prayer. He had to resist His soul and stay strong in His spirit for the will of God to be accomplished.

> *And He said, Abba, Father, all things are possible unto Thee; take away this cup from Me: nevertheless not what I will, but what Thou wilt* (Mark 14:36).

This is why Jesus said, "If possible let this cup pass from Me, yet not My will be done but Yours." He was speaking to His Heavenly Father from His spirit and not letting His mind pull Him off course. His soul was trying to pull Him in a different direction than His spirit. Yet, Jesus rose up in His spirit, yielding to God's purposes. He made His body and soul submit to His spirit, which was submitted to the will of God. The result was that He fulfilled the will of God for His life and for humanity.

Jesus won the spiritual tug-of-war that we often face, which tries to pull us from our time of prayer. He won the battle that tries to come between the spirit, soul, and body. We can learn how to rise up in our spirits and not give in to the pressure from our souls by His example. This is how we can also win the battle that tries to rage against our spiritual lives through Spiritual A.D.D.

SPIRITUAL A.D.D.

If you rise up in your spirit, you will win the spiritual tug-of-war because the spirit is stronger than the soul and flesh. This is why the same principle that worked for Jesus in the Garden will work for you and will break off the symptoms of Spiritual A.D.D. When you understand how powerful your spirit is to dominate the rest of your person, you can then keep your mind from wandering, and you will begin to enjoy your spiritual life with God.

> *So I say, live by the Spirit, and you will not gratify the desires of the sinful nature. For the sinful nature desires what is contrary to the Spirit, and the Spirit what is contrary to the sinful nature. They are in conflict with each other, so that you do not do what you want* (Galatians 5:16-17 NIV).

You just need to learn to develop your spiritual life, making your soul and flesh submit to the things of the spirit.

This same principle can further be prophetically applied to us today as we look at the Scripture when Jesus rode into Jerusalem on a donkey (see Luke 19:30). Why did Jesus ride a donkey? Perhaps one reason was because the donkey represents our stubborn fleshly nature, our minds that want to wander and rebel against the things of God. It represents the carnal nature that must be submitted to the ways of God. The Bible says that people are born into the earth with natures like wild donkeys. *"For vain man would be wise, though man be born like a wild ass's colt"* (Job 11:12). This means that we are born into this earth with a fleshly nature that is resistant to spiritual things and stubborn against God.

This is why we need to be born again spiritually and continue to walk in the spirit and not fulfill the stubborn desires of our flesh. Jesus riding in on a donkey prophetically reveals to us that our flesh nature needs to submit to His Lordship and life in the Spirit. When we are submitted, we will always overcome the flesh that wants to resist spiritual things. We can see this in the fact that Jesus rode on a donkey that had never been ridden before.

> *Saying, Go ye into the village over against you; in the which at your entering ye shall find a colt tied, whereon yet never man sat: loose him, and bring him hither* (Luke 19:30).

Can you imagine trying to ride a wild donkey that had never been ridden? It would most likely kick, resist, and act stubbornly with the rider. This is indeed a picture of our stubborn souls and flesh that need to submit to the things of God. It also reveals to us the need for the Lordship of Jesus in our lives to help us submit our stubborn souls and flesh, which want to go contrary to the way and life of the spirit. This is the tug-of-war—the spirit against the flesh. Our spirits try to pull us into the things of God, and our flesh tries to pull us into the things of this world and away from God. This is exactly what Spiritual A.D.D. does.

I have learned an important principle regarding winning at this tug-of-war and enjoying a more fulfilled life with God. Whatever we feed the most, making it the strongest, will ultimately win out. To better illustrate this point, I will share a tug-of-war challenge from my childhood. I wasn't a very big kid, and there was this one kid whom my friends and I would challenge to a game of tug-of-war. He was bigger than all of us, so it was the "little" kids against just one big kid. We would pull and pull to no avail, and he would beat us every time because he was stronger, bigger, and more dominant.

This same principle will help us overcome Spiritual A.D.D.: Whatever is the biggest in our lives will win, and will dominate us, just like that big kid dominated us little kids. It really is pretty simple. If we feed on spiritual things, we will be spiritually strong! The opposite is also true. If we feed on fleshly, worldly, natural things and give little attention to our spiritual lives, we will lose the war every time. The more we feed on spiritual things and guard our minds, the easier it is to defeat the Spiritual A.D.D. that wants to pull us away, tugging at us to resist the things of God.

When we set our hearts and minds toward spiritual things, the result will often be a battle to stay focused, interested, and engaged. This is because of the tug-of-war going on between our spirits and our flesh. It comes down to the principle that whatever we feed the most will determine the direction of our spiritual lives. This is how Spiritual A.D.D. works to get us distracted, to get our minds wandering, to get us tired and procrastinating in order to keep us from reaching the place of spiritual strength.

When your spirit is hungry for the things of God, you need to feed it. There is a healthy craving and lusting in your spirit. Have you ever felt the desire to pray, to shut off the television, or you just couldn't wait until you got home to be with God? This happens because your spirit is lusting for spiritual things.

> *This I say then, Walk in the Spirit, and ye shall not fulfil the lust of the flesh. For the flesh lusteth against the Spirit, and the Spirit against the flesh...* (Galatians 5:16-17).

To win the tug-of-war between your flesh and your spirit, it is helpful to obey the lusts of your spirit while starving your flesh. How do you do that? When you have that craving to read your Bible, pray, or go to church— go ahead and do it joyfully with all of your heart. This will feed the lust of your spirit, which is craving for God and things of the spiritual life that it needs. Your flesh will try to resist you and pull you away from spiritual things. You have to determine you aren't going to be pulled away into Spiritual A.D.D., but instead are going to resist it and obey your spiritual desires to do the things of God willfully and joyfully. This is one of the best ways to defeat Spiritual A.D.D. and win the tug-of-war between your soul and spirit.

Here is a brief list of things you can consider if you want to rise up in your spirit, dominate your soul, and increase your spiritual hunger. Taking note of these things can help you win over the effects of Spiritual A.D.D.:

- Turn off cell phones or other phones so you won't be distracted by calls during prayer.

- Turn off the computer or spend time with God away from the distractions of one.

- Play worship music while you pray or read to help you concentrate.

- Include spiritual things in your day-to-day routine, staying consistent so you will crave spiritual things and starve your flesh.

- Find a quiet place or create one to concentrate on God.

- Find a time that is best suited for concentrating on the Lord

- Try abstaining from or cutting back on unnecessary things that steal from your time with God and affect your spiritual hunger.

- Make a list of things you need to do before you pray or before you go to bed so that while you are praying or reading, you are focused.

- Write down a prayer list and try to avoid letting your mind wander in thinking about other things.

- Use the Spiritual ABC's at the beginning of your prayer time: Try coming up with a descriptive attribute of God for each letter of the alphabet. For example: A is for Awesome, B is for Beautiful, C is for Caring. This helps you to focus and concentrate on God, keeping your mind from wandering.

After reading these tips, did you see some areas in your life that would be helpful to adjust? As you can see, many of these things are simple adjustments that can make a huge difference in winning the race of your mind. You just need to pull the reins on your mind by watching for things that try to distract you, causing you to wander and allowing Spiritual A.D.D. to take root.

Many can relate to the tug-of-war that tries to affect their spiritual walk and the struggle that often happens when they go to pray, read the Bible, go to church, or just spend good quality time with God. Their minds begin to wander, and they become easily distracted, eventually talking themselves out of spending time doing spiritual things. In just about anything, our approach in the first few minutes of a particular task will make or break our success. This is true in spiritual things as well: Our minds can begin to wander or be bombarded with all kinds of thoughts of things that we should be doing rather than spending time around the things of God. These thoughts can be positive or negative and often determine the quality of our spiritual pursuit of godly things. Our minds tend to race with all kinds of things that we need to accomplish or would rather be doing.

Your mind will always try to challenge you. It does this by throwing doubts, fears, worries, and anxieties at you to try to distract you or cause you to quit. This is why, as I mentioned before, you need to learn to put the reins on your soul and win the spiritual tug-of-war. However you respond to the thoughts and things that are trying to hinder you will determine the outcome of your spiritual time with God.

Have you ever noticed that the minute you decide you are going to pray, you start thinking about whether you took out the garbage or completed other tasks? The specifics are different for everyone, but most people can probably attest to the sudden thoughts that try to distract them while they are having their devotions. Something I suggest to help keep the mind from wanting to wander is to make a list before you go to bed. You can also do this with the things you want to pray about as you enter into prayer. It's what I call clearing the mind and getting focused. It helps me to be more organized, keeps my mind from wandering, and enables me to put my heart into what I am doing.

Put Your Whole Heart Into It

When you put your heart into something, you are submitting your will like Jesus did in the Garden of Gethsemane (see Mark 14:35-36). You are saying, "I will do this!" It is the power of your will. This is why, as we mentioned before, speaking to yourself is so important to defeating Spiritual A.D.D.

Putting your heart into something is vital—it accesses the power of your will. This was demonstrated by lucifer, the devil, (though obviously in a negative way) when he tried to overthrow God and His Kingdom. The Bible records five times in Isaiah 14:13-14 that lucifer purposed with his whole heart to try to rebel against God. Five times he said, "I will..." in reference to his attempt to steal God's authority. He spoke to himself what his heart's purpose was, and he submitted his will to do it. He put his whole heart and determination into thinking he could overthrow God. We know the result: Because of those "I will's," which revealed his twisted heart, he was kicked out of Heaven.

SPIRITUAL A.D.D.

We obviously should not emulate the devil's rebellion, but we can learn from his wholeheartedness in this example. In a good and positive way, we can defeat Spiritual A.D.D. by speaking our hearts' intents and submitting our spirits to God's purposes. This comes by us saying, "I will…" in accordance with the plan of God. When we do, we will defeat the devil, who uses Spiritual A.D.D. to his advantage, still seeking to overthrow God's Kingdom by distracting His children.

We can rise up and address our minds and the devil, who tries to attack our thoughts and make our spiritual lives miserable. We don't have to suffer or feel defeated. Instead, we can place our hands over minds, praying and claiming the benefits that Jesus paid for with His blood. Jesus paid for our minds to be blessed by redeeming us with His own blood. When He died on the cross, He became sin so we in exchange could become the righteousness of God in Christ (see 2 Cor. 5:21). In the same way, we exchanged our carnal minds, mental attacks, Spiritual A.D.D., depression, and the like for His thoughts and a renewed mind.

Because of the blood of Jesus, we can say we now have the mind of Christ. *"For who hath known the mind of the Lord, that he may instruct Him? But we have the mind of Christ"* (1 Cor. 2:16). This means we can have renewed minds and proper thoughts.

How did we obtain this mind of Christ? At His crucifixion, Jesus wore a crown of thorns, which was literally slammed onto His head. When the soldiers did this to Him, something glorious took place for you and me—the purchasing of our minds to be blessed and renewed. Those thorns were a picture of the redeeming blood that He shed, which is a hedge of protection over our thoughts. As the soldiers mocked Jesus, putting the crown of thorns on His head, the devil had no clue that this action was giving us a new, powerful weapon against him.

We now have available to us this powerful blood of Jesus that renews and protects our minds against the devil's attacks. This means that our minds don't have to be garbage pails for the junk of this earth or open doors for the enemy's distracting thoughts. Our minds have been purchased by the precious blood of Jesus! However, because we live in this world and our minds are affected every day, we need to renew our minds through God's Word and presence. We need to put a spiritual rein on our minds that will help us keep our thoughts subject to the knowledge of God. We can do this through the power of Jesus' blood and through putting our whole hearts into seeking Him.

I pray you are seeing just how powerful your spirit is and how important it is to submit your will to Him. As you have been reading, I hope you have seen the success in your spiritual life that can be obtained to defeat

SPIRITUAL A.D.D.

Spiritual A.D.D. This success is especially possible when you are doing things with all your heart. Putting your heart into something is all about choice. It is called *heart attitude*, and it keeps your mind from getting in the way of your time with God. Defeating Spiritual A.D.D. and having an enjoyable spiritual life usually comes down to a few decisions and steps. It often comes down to the distance of just a few inches—the distance between your head and your heart.

Jesus pointed this out in Mark chapter 12 when He told a scribe that he was not far from the Kingdom of God. He said this after seeing him intelligently answer His question regarding what is the greatest commandment. *"When Jesus saw that he had answered intelligently, He said to him, 'You are not far from the kingdom of God'..."* (Mark 12:34 NASB). This man had the right answer from his head, but it wasn't from his heart. He answered intelligently—but without the revelation of it in his heart. As a result, Jesus told him he wasn't far from the Kingdom of God.

Some of us may be exactly that close to a spiritual breakthrough from Spiritual A.D.D.—the ever-so-important distance between our heads and our hearts. Sometimes it comes down to just those few inches, those small decisions or steps that can cause our spiritual lives to be productive (or not). Unless we make the spiritual decision to approach our walk with God with our whole hearts, it starts to become routine, rehearsed, boring, and unfulfilling. This happens when we stop putting our hearts into it and let our minds or other things dictate the level of our spiritual pursuit of God. Putting our whole hearts into God, prayer, Bible reading, and other spiritual activities, as well as having the right attitude, helps immensely.

Wholeheartedness keeps us from becoming negative or frustrated, and it requires of us the right attitudes and focus. Spiritual A.D.D. is about the heart and can be cured by having the right heart attitude. As I mentioned before, it is vastly important that our spirits, or hearts, are the predominant aspect of our selves that we are strengthening. When our hearts are in it, everything else in our lives will fall into proper order and spiritual fulfillment.

Jesus pointed out this principle when He quoted the greatest commandment of all.

> *And thou shalt love the Lord thy God with all thy heart, and with all thy soul, and with all thy mind, and with all thy strength: this is the first commandment* (Mark 12:30).

He mentions first loving God with *all* our hearts. This is because, when we put our whole hearts into seeking Him and the things of God, we are set on the right path for blessings.

SPIRITUAL A.D.D.

One person who sought God with his whole heart was King David. *"With my whole heart have I sought Thee..."* (Ps. 119:10). The Bible reveals why he was so blessed and loved by the Lord—he was a man after God's heart (see Acts 13:22). He sought the Lord with all his heart and put Him first, even in the midst of sin, struggles, and enemies. What worked for King David will work for you!

I cannot emphasize how important it is to stay focused in your spiritual life—striving to put your whole heart into time in the Bible, prayer, worship, going to church, and spending time with God. When you focus and don't let your mind wander, when you really put your heart into it, God is ready to respond. He wants to, as shown in the Book of Ezekiel.

And the man said to me, Son of man, look with your eyes and hear with your ears, and set your heart and mind on all that I will show you, for you are brought here so that I may show them to you... (Ezekiel 40:4 AMP).

God was telling Ezekiel, through an angelic messenger, to stay focused. He told him to do this by looking with his eyes and expecting to hear with his spiritual ears. If he would also stay focused in his mind and not let it wander, God would respond by showing things to him.

This is exactly true for us. A good way to do this is to close our eyes in prayer, unless of course we are driving.

Another thing we can do is try to shut off the noise and distractions around us so we can better focus. Jesus knew the importance of this, and He told us to shut the door when we pray.

> *But thou, when thou prayest, enter into thy closet, and when thou hast shut thy door, pray to thy Father which is in secret; and thy Father which seeth in secret shall reward thee openly* (Matthew 6:6).

The Lord was telling us in this verse to get ourselves into a place where God is our focus. He was telling us how to shut off and shut out other things that will distract us. Sometimes we have to shut off the thoughts that are trying to bombard our minds and break our focus from spiritual things.

Let It Flow From the Heart

One of the great ways to shut off the distractions is to flow from your heart by connecting to God with your human spirit, or what is commonly called your heart (not your natural heart but your spiritual heart). It is that place deep inside that is the real you, the place where real gut decisions are made.

Jesus referenced the heart's location when He mentioned the baptism of the Holy Spirit.

SPIRITUAL A.D.D.

Anyone who believes in Me may come and drink! For the Scriptures declare, "Rivers of living water will flow from his heart." (When He said "living water," He was speaking of the Spirit, who would be given to everyone believing in Him. But the Spirit had not yet been given, because Jesus had not yet entered into His glory) (John 7:38-39 NLT).

In the King James Version of this verse, it says, "*... Out of his belly shall flow rivers of living water*" (John 7:38). These Scriptures are important in helping us understand the need to do things for the Lord with our whole hearts.

These verses also show another principle that helps us overcome Spiritual A.D.D. They reveal another way to shut the door of our minds and empower us to connect with God, spirit-to-Spirit. This powerful tool is called *praying in the Spirit* and is especially helpful when we don't know what to pray about, or our minds are wandering and want to dominate our lives.

In the same way the Spirit also helps our weakness; for we do not know how to pray as we should, but the Spirit Himself intercedes for us with groanings too deep for words (Romans 8:26 NASB).

Sometimes we don't know how to pray for something or don't know what to pray about, so God has provided a way, in addition to the prayers we utter with our understanding. Prayer in the Spirit doesn't come from our minds but rather from our hearts (our spirits).

What is powerful about this is that it lets the Holy Spirit pray through us. He gives us the utterances to speak (see Acts 2:4). We don't have to try to form them or come up with them in our minds, but rather they are inspired by the Holy Spirit. Our job is to just yield to these expressions and utterances as we open our mouths and let Him pray through us, giving us the words to pray in the Spirit. We don't have to try and figure out every word or the perfect way to formulate the words. Yes, we are doing the speaking; it is our words and our voice, but the utterances come from God to our spirits for us to then pray out.

We pray in the Spirit as we yield to Him in our spirits. God has provided this option so our minds won't get in the way and we can pray, connecting to God with our spirits. Our minds may want to wander, but the power of God and the ability of our spirits to connect to the Lord is greater than our minds. When praying in the Spirit, direct communication is taking place between our spirits and God's Spirit. The Bible also says that when we pray in the Spirit, our minds are unfruitful as our spirits pray (see 1 Cor. 14:14). It is unfruitful because our spirits are praying, not our heads. This is extremely powerful, especially when we don't know how to pray about something or have been struggling to focus in our times of prayer. Those are perfect times to pray in the Spirit.

SPIRITUAL A.D.D.

The ability to pray in the Spirit is a promise Jesus gave for us today. On the day of Pentecost, Peter said this promise was for those there in Jerusalem that day, for their children, and for those who are far off.

> *Then Peter said unto them, Repent, and be baptized every one of you in the name of Jesus Christ for the remission of sins, and ye shall receive the gift of the Holy Ghost. For the promise is unto you, and to your children, and to all that are afar off, even as many as the LORD our God shall call* (Acts 2:38-39).

The requirement for being able to pray in the Spirit is that we first have to be saved as Christians (see John 3). Then there is an additional experience known as the baptism of the Holy Spirit, which gives us power (see John 7:37-39; Acts 1:8). At the back of this book, I have included a prayer and instructions on how to receive this infilling for those who are Christians but have not received the baptism of the Spirit.

This powerful tool God provided helps us defeat Spiritual A.D.D. because with it we are praying from our spirits. We aren't letting our minds pull us from spiritual things but are connecting to God in our spirits. The beauty of this is that we can seek God both by praying with our understanding, as the apostle Paul teaches in First Corinthians, and in the spirit also!

> *What is the outcome then? I will pray with the spirit and I will pray with the mind also; I will sing with the*

spirit and I will sing with the mind also (1 Corinthians 14:15 NASB).

Praying in the Spirit, when done regularly, is an amazing way to keep you focused. It builds you up spiritually, aiding in the strength of your Christian walk. Helping you win the race of your mind, it is extremely powerful if you are suffering with the symptoms of Spiritual A.D.D. Rather than trying to focus on one thing you have to do or a number of steps that are helpful and important, you can simply focus on one exercise—praying in the Spirit—that will build you and reconnect you with God. It is a great way to get you back into the game spiritually. It helps you to put your foot down in the spirit and win that race of the mind. It is one way to help you "keep your feet"!

Keep Your Feet

What does it mean to keep your feet? *"Keep your foot [give your mind to what you are doing] when you go [as Jacob to sacred Bethel] to the house of God..."* (Eccl. 5:1 AMP). This verse in the Amplified Bible says that you "keep your foot" by giving your mind, or attention, to what you are doing. This verse is telling you to stay focused and balanced, to hold your position, and to think through your thoughts and actions prayerfully. When you keep your foot in the things of God, you aren't letting your mind wander and race all over the place.

SPIRITUAL A.D.D.

Discipline and action are required on your part to pull the reins on your mind by guarding your thoughts. You can take that determined step in your spirit to defeat Spiritual A.D.D. You just need to tighten things up and not let your mind take you on a journey into a path of Spiritual A.D.D.

The Bible calls tightening things up in our minds and not letting them wander loosely "girding up" our minds. *"Wherefore gird up the loins of your mind, be sober..."* (1 Pet. 1:13). The word "girding" in this verse means to tighten, to take up slack, and to prepare our minds for action. *"Therefore, prepare your minds for action..."* (1 Pet. 1:13 NASB). Are we ready to prepare our minds for action? The verse continues by telling us how to do it—by staying alert and fixing our hope on the grace of God given to us. *"...Keep sober in spirit, fix your hope completely on the grace to be brought to you at the revelation of Jesus Christ"* (1 Pet. 1:13 NASB). Sounds like keeping our feet, doesn't it?

Are you ready to win the race of the mind? Are you getting determined to put the reins on your mind and to posses your soul? Remember, you can win the tug-of-war that wants to pull you into a life of Spiritual A.D.D. because you have the power of God in you! All Christians have that power available in their born-again spirits to bring their thoughts into order. We have been granted the ability to get results by praying both in the Spirit and with our understanding. This enables us to stand strong and "keep our feet" in whatever we do for the Lord. We can do it with *all* our might! This is the lasting joy and results that every true believer wants, especially a life that wins against Spiritual A.D.D. Be encouraged to win against it and to finish your spiritual race strong, victorious, and refreshed as you pursue Him. Don't let your mind get in the way of your spiritual life; you have so many things provided by the Lord to help you win! Are you ready? Start pulling those reins!

Endnote

1. James Strong, *The New Strong's Exhaustive Concordance of the Bible* (Nashville, TN: Thomas Nelson, 1991), Hebrew #1288.

Chapter Four

PAYING ATTENTION
COSTS TOO MUCH

Keep your eyes straight ahead; ignore all sideshow distractions (Proverbs 4:25 MSG).

Early one morning I headed to my prayer room to begin my time with the Lord. I had my Bible in one hand and my hot cup of coffee in the other. I turned the lamp on in my room, took a few sips from my coffee cup, and read a few Scriptures. However, across the room something kept catching my eye, distracting me. I got up and headed to that side of the room. There it was right before my eyes! I could hardly believe it! No, it wasn't Jesus, an angel, or anything else spiritual, but rather it was a model train that I had been working on for a few days.

Perhaps you are wondering, *Why would you be distracted by a model train?* I have had a love for model trains ever since I was a young child and have been an avid collector for years. I have been building my train layout for many years, and it's something I really enjoy. In fact, I was enjoying it too much, and this routine of going to my prayer room and working on this train lasted for a few days. It seemed every morning for a few days, while I should have been praying, spending time with God, I would get distracted and get up and work on that train.

That happened *until* something else happened that I wasn't expecting. I heard a voice speak to me—a very loving, but firm voice that dropped me to my knees. This voice said to me, "Hank, lovest thou Me more than trains?" *Great*, I thought as I was on my knees, convicted and feeling like the kid who got caught by his mom with his hand in the cookie jar. I knew this voice was the Lord speaking to me about being distracted by this train, but I wondered, *Did He have to say it in King James Version?* He spoke it again, "Hank, lovest thou Me more than trains?" I thought, *Are You kidding me, God? This sounds like what You said to Peter in the Bible, when You asked him if he loved You more than natural things.* "So when they had dined, Jesus saith to Simon Peter, Simon, son of Jonas, lovest thou Me more than these?" (John 21:15). *Of course, I love You more than trains.* It didn't take long for me to repent for letting this train distract me and pull me from my time with God.

I got a glimpse that day of just how jealous and excited God is about our time with Him. He waits for it and cherishes it. I was letting that train come between God and me, and the Lord wasn't pleased about it. It wasn't that He was bothered so much by the train but rather by me being distracted. I took my eyes or focus off of Him and became distracted by something else. As I was on my knees telling the Lord that I did love Him more than the train, I also began to laugh as I realized that the Lord is such a good God and Father. He has such a sense of humor—quoting it to me in the King James Version by saying, "Lovest thou Me more than these?" I haven't heard anyone use the word lovest in our modern language when they talk. I knew the Lord was being funny with me, and it certainly got my attention, stopping this daily distraction.

Distractions, Distractions, Distractions

Does this story about my train distraction sounds familiar to your life? Maybe you are having your own set of things that are pulling you away from quality time with God or spiritual things. Maybe you are dealing with Spiritual A.D.D. and don't know what to do.

SPIRITUAL A.D.D.

Whatever they may be, we must not allow these distractions to take our eyes off of the Lord and steal our time with Him (like with my train). Staying focused and minimizing or removing distractions is necessary for overcoming Spiritual A.D.D. We need to keep our focus on God and stay consistent in our prayer and Bible reading time. It is so easy in this day and age to take our eyes off the Lord and focus on the waves of things coming at us or even the storms of life.

This is exactly what happened to Peter. He was being groomed by Jesus to become a powerful leader, but he got distracted. The Lord, after feeding the multitudes, told Peter to get in the boat ahead of Him with the other disciples. Then something happened that Peter and the others didn't expect. A wind began to cause the waves and the sea to toss their boat like it was a toy. The disciples were panicking with fear, but Jesus miraculously walked upon the water toward them. They were so afraid at the events they were experiencing that they didn't recognize that it was the Lord. They thought He was a ghost instead.

> *When the disciples saw Him walking on the lake, they were terrified. "It's a ghost," they said, and cried out in fear. But Jesus immediately said to them: "Take courage! It is I. Don't be afraid"* (Matthew 14:26-27 NIV).

After hearing Jesus calling out to them, Peter began questioning if it was really the Lord who was walking on the water toward them. He asked Jesus, if it was Him, to ask him to come to Him on the water. The Lord responded by telling Peter to go ahead and get out of the boat and walk to Him on the water. However, as he got out of the boat and started to walk on the water by God's supernatural power, Peter quickly became distracted as fear of the wind and waves gripped him. This caused him to lose focus from the Lord, and he began to sink, crying out for the Lord to save him.

Of course, the Lord did save him, but imagine what would have happened if he had kept his eyes on the Lord. He wouldn't have sunk! This is true for many who suffer and are feeling as though their spiritual lives are sinking fast, like Peter. This is because the symptoms of Spiritual A.D.D. can make it difficult to focus on spiritual things without being distracted. Its purpose is to get our eyes and pursuit off the Lord, like Peter, and onto the things around us. Then we won't accomplish the things we desire.

Peter would have been fine had he kept his focus on the Lord and resisted the distractions around him. His own mind began to pull him from his spiritual focus, causing him to sink because he got distracted. This is so easy to do without realizing that it is happening. I like how The Message Bible tells us to avoid these things. It tells us to avoid sideshow distractions that will get our focus off of the Lord. *"Keep your eyes straight ahead; ignore all sideshow distractions"* (Prov. 4:25 MSG).

These sideshow distractions can come from many different sources, and they are different for each person. For Peter, it was the water and the wind; for me, it was my train. Take a moment to reflect. What is it in your life that may be distracting you? What things are trying to keep you from focusing on God?

For some, admitting to anything might be hard, while others have a list a mile long. Truth be known, many Christians, even the most disciplined ones, including leaders and pastors, have all had to deal with plenty of sideshow type distractions in this modern world of technology. There are plenty of things in this earth to distract us and aid in the symptoms of Spiritual A.D.D. The enemy's goal is to get our focus off the things of God and onto other things around us, making them sideshow distractions. These distractions can include e-mails, Facebook, Twitter, the Internet, cell phones, family, friends, sports, hobbies, entertainment, work, and many other things.

These sideshow distractions may not be necessarily bad and may even be necessary. Yet, we can't let them pull us from our spiritual pursuit of God—to the point that we prioritize them or get distracted by them more than the things of God. Unfortunately, we can't always control or avoid these. Yet, we still need to learn how to not let them dictate or affect our walk with God or our time with Him.

A good way to help determine if Spiritual A.D.D. is affecting us in the form of distractions is to better understand what defines something as being a distraction. *Distraction* by definition means to draw apart or bring a separation. It is that which diverts our attention or a diversion. It is a state in which our attention is called in different ways by confusion, perplexity, or disorder. Once we discover what a distraction is, we recognize more easily how it can work against us in our spiritual lives. Distractions are meant to get us to give our full attention to something else. This often occurs while we are pursuing the things of God. These distractions, whether good or bad, are meant to prevent us from doing what we want to or should be doing for the Lord. If we are experiencing these things, we are probably distracted and are dealing with a form of Spiritual A.D.D.

It is important to understand that distractions affect many Christians and can be remedied with a few adjustments in our lives. However, part of the process of overcoming them is the willingness to recognize that we are being distracted. Then we must find the discipline to make the necessary adjustments so we don't become distracted and so that we know how to deal with distractions if they should arise.

If they are not addressed within our lives, they can cause us to lose our desire, focus, and attention for the Lord or spiritual things. When this happens, we can become frustrated, which causes our prayer lives to struggle. We start losing interest in the things of God, which causes a downward spiral. This can result in our walk with God seeming like it is spinning out of control at times. Day after day, we find ourselves struggling to focus on the things of God. We find it harder to stay interested in our spiritual lives, sometimes even leaving our times with God feeling unfulfilled.

Does this sound familiar to you and what you might be dealing with? I want you to be encouraged because this isn't the way things have to be. As I mentioned before, distractions are one of the main symptoms of Spiritual A.D.D., and when they're trying to run wild in your life, they can be lassoed. One way to rein them in and avoid these pesky distractions, distractions, distractions, is to take note of the things that often try to distract you.

Taking Note of Distractions

You can take note of distractions by writing them down or making note of them. You accomplish this by considering your daily routine, interruptions, and other things you may have scheduled. Ask yourself, *How are these things influencing my spiritual life?* In other words, if it is your computer that is distracting you, take note of it. Is it pulling you from your time with God by excessive Facebooking, e-mailing, Internet searching and shopping, and the like—especially when you are trying to spend time with God? Are your devotions often interrupted, or do you rarely find time for them because you have to check your computer or look at the phone to see who may have texted?

When we take note of the subtle and obvious things trying to interrupt and steal our time, we will better deal with Spiritual A.D.D. When we take note of something, it doesn't mean just recognizing the things distracting us; it is also means choosing to do something about it. For example, we could choose to turn the cell phone off while praying or choose to spend time with God instead of surfing the Internet or watching television all night.

We need to make note of what things are being pesky distractions that are stealing our time from the Lord. It is liberating when we come to realize that we don't have to answer our phones just because we carry them on us, even while we are in prayer. We need to be able to have the discipline to turn them off and not always treat them like they are crying newborns. (I personally don't like cell phones because people often expect others to always answer their calls or texts simply because they have their phones with them.)

SPIRITUAL A.D.D.

Often the reason some deal with Spiritual A.D.D. in the form of distractions is because of poor time discipline and time management. We are told in Scripture that we are to use our time wisely, *"Making the most of your time, because the days are evil"* (Eph. 5:16 NASB). This means we are to fight distraction. The problem with Spiritual A.D.D. in the form of distractions is that it takes up time and energy that can produce a satisfied spiritual walk with God. This is why we are told to watch or pay attention to our time and how it is being used.

As we have seen, distractions can easily be fixed if we will take note of what is distracting us and stealing our time. This comes by proper time management and establishing the right priorities. Computers, cell phones, television, and other modern conveniences can actually become inconveniences if we are not careful. They can be enjoyable, but we need to take note of how they are affecting us in our spiritual walk. Are they helping us or hindering us by becoming distractions that are getting out of control, putting our spiritual lives on the back burner?

Something else we need to take note of is how much time is being stolen from us because of these unwanted or unneeded distractions. If the time we are losing is significant, we may need to consider how to better plan out our days and weeks—making sure we purposely schedule, prioritize, and guard the things of God. The more organized and orderly we are, the more difficult it is for distractions to take us off course. In the end, organization leads to a healthy spiritual life and helps to overcome Spiritual A.D.D.

You may be thinking, *But I have tried some of these things, and I am still distracted. I feel like Spiritual A.D.D. is running my life.* If this is you, keep something in mind. You have to keep working at your spiritual life, refusing to give up. As I have highlighted throughout this book, your heart must be involved in your spiritual pursuit. It always comes down to you having a real heart check and commitment. This is especially true if you want to bring Spiritual A.D.D. and distractions under control. If you want to change, (you guessed it!) it will require you to not be halfhearted! Your heart attitude and commitment is so important in winning the battle against Spiritual A.D.D.

I have found true in my life the importance of putting my heart into the things of God. In over 25 years of serving God, I have noticed that when I am feeling distracted in prayer or Bible reading, which occurs from time to time, it is usually because I am approaching this time halfheartedly. However, once I take note of it with a simple heart adjustment and time management, it is remedied and things return to proper order and balance in my life.

Let me give you an example of what I mean by putting my heart into something and not getting distracted.

SPIRITUAL A.D.D.

Jesus knew the importance of getting away to pray without being distracted. He was often seen withdrawing Himself from the crowds and the many distractions that constantly pulled on Him in order to spend time with the Father. *"And He withdrew Himself into the wilderness, and prayed"* (Luke 5:16). I decided to follow the Lord's example and get away to pray. I figured that if it worked for Him, it would work for me! I was all ready to meet with God and spend a weekend away from my family seeking the Lord in a prayer cabin. I was determined that all I would bring with me was clothes, a sleeping bag, a Bible, a notebook, and some water. *These are going to be the best days of my spiritual life,* I thought. Right? Wrong!

It started off great, as my spiritual adrenaline began to kick in and I determined I would suffer for Jesus. I prayed at first so long, hard, and fervently. I read my Bible for several hours, until I started to get antsy. I found myself constantly getting up, looking out the window, going outside for a moment, and then walking back inside to more of the Spiritual A.D.D. symptoms that joined my prayer getaway. I lay down, then got up, then walked and prayed, then kneeled and prayed. I was starting to really get fidgety and bored, feeling like I was experiencing cabin fever. Yet, I hadn't been there that long, maybe a few hours.

I looked at my watch as it seemed to be moving so slowly and for eternity. I had no cell phone, radio, music, or outside modern technology to enjoy. I was suffering and miserable. It felt like I had been there for days! It was so bad I finally got in my car and went back into town to get a hamburger. What I didn't realize was how much I had gotten used to all the things around me as a regular part of my life and routine. Once they were removed, I went into withdrawal, so to speak. We are so used to a fast-paced society that we often don't realize how much all the things that we have and that surround us affect our spiritual walk, attitudes, and fervor. Now, I am much better and can handle things better than I did then, but that time taught me some things.

Does this story sound familiar in your spiritual life? If it does, I encourage you to take note of things that may be trying to pull you from needed time with God. I often try really hard in my prayer times to take note of possible distractions. I do this by choosing to turn off my phone, my computer, and outside distractions, and focus solely on the Lord, putting my whole heart and attention to what I am doing.

Let's look at what David said about his pursuit with God and how he dealt with distractions. He gave us a clue of what will help us to avoid distractions.

> *With my whole heart have I sought Thee: O let me not wander from Thy commandments. Thy word have I hid in mine heart, that I might not sin against Thee* (Psalm 119:10-11).

— 115 —

David made a clear connection between having a focused heart and not being distracted. He said this was a vital step so he could seek God with his whole heart. It would then, in return, help him not to wander or be distracted. He also mentioned the importance of the Word of God in keeping him focused. This is an important thing to implement in our lives and is helpful for dealing with Spiritual A.D.D.

We can pray the Word of God out loud to help us better focus and not become distracted. When we speak the Word of God out loud by reading, memorizing, or praying the Word, it does minimize distractions. The Bible is so powerful that it actually engages us when we speak it. There is something about our ears hearing us speak the Word of God out loud that has powerful results and will keep us focused. If we will give it a try or do it more often, we will see amazing results!

The Needful Thing

As I mentioned before, distractions affect everyone differently and are different for everyone. Sometimes distractions are a result of being too busy. It may not be bad or evil things that are keeping us busy, but they still limit us in spiritual things. Parenting, school, jobs, recreation, hobbies, sports, leisure—the list can go on and on—can keep us busy and can get us distracted from spiritual things. If we don't establish some kind of order with them, these things will further promote Spiritual A.D.D. They aren't evil distractions, but we have to consider how they are affecting our spiritual lives. This is an important step if we really want to change and not become distracted from having a healthy spiritual life with God.

The danger for all of us is to fall prey to the busyness of life so that we hinder our spiritual walk, thinking we are doing OK. This is what happened to a woman named Martha in the Bible, who became distracted by her own busyness. She thought she was doing the right thing when Jesus came to dinner at the house where she and her sister, Mary, lived. Martha was busy getting everything ready and perfect while Mary sat at Jesus' feet listening to Him.

> *Her sister, Mary, sat at the Lord's feet, listening to what He taught. But Martha was distracted by the big dinner she was preparing. She came to Jesus and said, "Lord, doesn't it seem unfair to You that my sister just sits here while I do all the work? Tell her to come and help me"* (Luke 10:39-40 NLT).

Yet, the Lord was not impressed with Martha's busyness, her choice to be distracted rather than spend time with Him. What she was doing wasn't necessarily bad or evil, but it wasn't needful at that time. Distractions can be good or bad, but nevertheless, they are distractions that affect our time with the Lord. Martha had a good distraction—she desperately wanted to serve the Lord properly by getting everything just right while Jesus visited her house. The problem was she got caught up in those sideshow distractions. She took her eyes off the Lord, just like Peter.

In contrast, her sister, Mary, got the Lord's attention because she was determined to focus on Jesus and not be distracted. She wasn't going to let distractions pull her from her "time with Jesus." We need to ask ourselves if distractions are pulling us away from spending time with the Lord like they were with Martha. It is obvious from this story that Jesus wants to be the highest, most important priority of our lives and days. We know this by the fact that He brought attention to Martha's distraction and failure to make Him her priority.

> *And Jesus answered and said unto her, Martha, Martha, thou art careful and troubled about many things: but one thing is needful: and Mary hath chosen that good part, which shall not be taken away from her* (Luke 10:41-42).

It is so easy, when dealing with Spiritual A.D.D., to become like Martha—distracted and easily pulled from spiritual things. Have you ever noticed how many distractions try to raise their ugly heads the moment you determine to spend time with God or get serious about your spiritual walk? As mentioned, you can also allow good things to become distractions, such as your family, finances, work, favorite programs, and hobbies, to name a few. These are important, however, if they are wrongly prioritized, they can become the most important things in your life, making your time with God less important.

That day at Martha's house, Jesus wanted her undivided attention; He wanted to be her priority. His desire hasn't changed. What would have happened if Martha had been more focused on spending time with the Lord instead of her preparations? She would have been more freed up to spend time with the Lord, and she wouldn't have been corrected by Him.

Jesus said that *one thing* is needful or should be the highest priority in our lives—spending time with Him and not being distracted. We have to watch and not allow Spiritual A.D.D. to take away our time with Him. The things we do every day can be needful in our minds and even necessary. However, the question we need to ask ourselves is, *Are they taking a greater priority than seeking first the Kingdom of God and His righteousness?* (see Matt. 6:33). Jesus was showing us that when it comes to God and our Christian spiritual walk, we must make God our highest priority and most "needful" thing. This is why King David said it was one thing that he desired and that was most important in his life.

> *One thing have I desired of the LORD, that will I seek after; that I may dwell in the house of the LORD all the*

> *days of my life, to behold the beauty of the LORD, and*
> *to enquire in His temple* (Psalm 27:4).

David shows us in this verse something that will help in overcoming Spiritual A.D.D. It is revealed in that verse as being *one thing!* This speaks of *time with God,* which is the most important thing that we must make our priority. It is exactly what Jesus said to Martha was the most needful thing in her life—desiring God above all else and not becoming distracted from Him. Making the Lord the *one thing* or *needful thing* requires focus, order, scheduling, and discipline on our parts. A helpful way to do this is to make it the first thing we do when we wake up and the last thing we do before retiring for the night; this is the recipe for a healthy spiritual life.

God also gave Joshua this instruction in the Bible, telling him to meditate on the Lord and the Scriptures both day and night.

> *Do not let this Book of the Law depart from your*
> *mouth; meditate on it day and night, so that you may*
> *be careful to do everything written in it. Then you will*
> *be prosperous and successful* (Joshua 1:8 NIV).

When you truly love the Lord, you will want to please Him and make Him a priority. Why not try scheduling into your day regular times to talk with God and read and meditate on Scripture? You will be glad you did because success and blessings, as this Scripture says, will come knocking on the door of your life!

Resisting Distractions

The Lord wants us to stay focused on Him, and the devil loves it when we are distracted from our time with God. This is why, when resisting distractions, we will often have to address the enemy who wants to steal our time with God and make our spiritual lives miserable and unproductive. He watches and knows the things that he can use to aid in distracting us. After all, this is how he gets a foothold. The Bible tells us to give him no place in our lives (see Eph. 4:27). When we do give him a place, he will even use Spiritual A.D.D. to his advantage, trying to gain a foothold.

Jesus warned in Scripture that the devil comes immediately to steal the seed of the Word of God in our lives.

> *And these are they by the way side, where the word is sown; but when they have heard, Satan cometh immediately, and taketh away the word that was sown in their hearts* (Mark 4:15).

We can see from this verse how the enemy is afraid of the people who set their hearts to be about God and obeying His Word. He comes immediately to try to affect our lives in a negative way. One such way is through Spiritual A.D.D. in the form of distractions. Not every distraction we face can be blamed on the devil, but he is determined to have his hand on most of them. In this same parable, the Lord mentions other things that can become distractions as well, causing our spiritual lives to be unproductive.

> *And these are they which are sown among thorns; such as hear the word, and the cares of this world, and the deceitfulness of riches, and the lusts of other things entering in, choke the word, and it becometh unfruitful* (Mark 4:18-19).

Take note of the things that Jesus said can cause us some frustrations or pain in the form of distractions and Spiritual A.D.D. He mentions three specific things that can choke out our spiritual lives, making them unfruitful. He tells us to be watchful of the cares of this world, the deceitfulness of riches, and the lust for other things. All three of these distractions try to keep us from having spiritual lives that are healthy and productive.

This is why we need to put a leash on Spiritual A.D.D., so to speak, and not let it dictate the direction we are going in our Christian walk. We have to do this so that we aren't being pulled in a direction that is opposite of spiritual productivity. We are advised by the apostle Paul in Scripture to turn away from distractions and things that can easily entangle us and to keep our eyes focused on the Lord instead (see Heb. 12:1-5).

This sounds like what happened to Peter when he tried walking on the water, or to Martha, who was more focused on her chores than the Lord. In both cases, they took their eyes off the Lord and got caught up in distractions instead. If we refuse to deal with Spiritual A.D.D. in the form of distractions, it may become a spiritual weight to us. This can cause us to become spiritually bored and to feel weighed down. Our minds can even become clouded, preventing us from a productive Christian life.

Many things can distract us from our spiritual lives and further cause us to struggle with Spiritual A.D.D.. They are different for everyone, yet, in most cases, they come down to three categories of distractions. I refer to these categories as *the danger of the noun*. A *noun*, according to definition, is a person, a place, or a thing. If these people, places, and things are not kept in proper balance, they can really hurt our spiritual walk and become major thorns of distractions.

This is what the Lord told Moses when He gave him instructions for the children of Israel. He mentioned some things to avoid as they crossed over the Jordan River into their land of inheritance. Just as they had a natural inheritance, we also have an inheritance—a spiritual inheritance that is in Christ and belongs to all Christians. Thus, the things God mentioned to the children of Israel in their natural inheritance prophetically apply to us spiritually today. The Lord warned them to beware of the "noun." He mentioned the three categories of distractions—people, places, and things:

> *Then ye shall drive out all the inhabitants of the land* [people] *from before you, and destroy all their pictures, and destroy all their molten images* [things], *and quite pluck down all their high places* [places] (Numbers 33:52).

The Lord was letting Israel know there were distractions waiting for them in the land of their inheritance. They were such things as the people who lived there, the high places of worship to false gods, and pictures and images used to worship these false gods. The Lord mentioned these things to keep Israel focused on Him as their God. However, He had to warn them of the effects these things could have on them if they became distracted and refused to eliminate them. He knew these could distract them, pulling them away from the Him.

> *But if ye will not drive out the inhabitants of the land from before you; then it shall come to pass, that those which ye let remain of them shall be pricks in your eyes, and thorns in your sides, and shall vex you in the land wherein ye dwell* (Numbers 33:55).

The failure to drive these things out of their lives could get them to lose focus and cause them a lot of problems. This is true for us if we don't deal with things trying to distract, or if we ignore Spiritual A.D.D.

The important thing for all of us is to be wise of these distractions and how they can be used to get our focus off of the Lord. Many of us are ready to go deeper with the Lord and want to be more aware of distractions. The question is: How do we go about our spiritual lives even if we are still feeling the weight of these distractions? I believe the way is pretty easy to apply. It's what I will refer to as *indentifying and addressing distractions.*

Identify and Address Distractions

Now that we have been made aware of how distractions can get us off course with the Lord, let's identify specific distractions and address them. That's right—we can address them! We don't have to tolerate those seemingly unmovable mountains of distraction and Spiritual A.D.D.

Jesus taught His disciples a powerful principle of how to address obstacles, and it will work for us today. He instructed His disciples in the importance of identifying and addressing obstacles. Jesus began by pointing to a literal mountain that they could see as they were walking with Him one particular day.

> *...For verily I say unto you, If ye have faith as a grain of mustard seed, ye shall say unto this mountain, Remove hence to yonder place; and it shall remove;*

and nothing shall be impossible unto you (Matthew 17:20).

We know that He was giving them a life lesson about a specific mountain because He said "this mountain." If we could speak to a literal mountain by faith and see it be removed, then what can we do with a mountain of distractions? Jesus points to this literal mountain to show us that no matter how big we think something is, if we identify specifically what it is, then we can address it, causing it to no longer stand in our way. Only if we are willing to take the necessary steps to identify and address it will we see the desired breakthrough we are seeking. This means that if Spiritual A.D.D. is hindering us and standing in our way, we have the answer to removing it!

The Lord is telling us in this Scripture not to tolerate those things that are hindering us or distracting us from our walk with Him. He wants us to have a different attitude instead of simply going around and around the same mountain of problems and distractions. Rather, He taught us to identify the mountain or distraction first so we can remove it. We do this by taking note of what distraction or obstacle is before us. Once we have identified it, then we follow the next step Jesus gave His disciples in that same verse—we address it.

We address it by speaking to the mountain of distractions or obstacles. In other words, by speaking to it, we are not tolerating or ignoring it. We are not going around it but addressing it by facing it head on! We are to address it by taking a place of commitment, determination, and command as we use our faith and authority in Christ to remove its ability to distract us. It is not difficult. We can identify and address our mountains or obstacles just like Jesus taught His disciples to do.

To get started, when you are ready to identify and address your obstacles, ask yourself some basic questions. The mountain image often describes how people feel when they are dealing with Spiritual A.D.D. They feel like their situations are mountains, huge and immovable. If that is how you feel, ask yourself some questions to better identify and address the distraction:

Do I need to stop what I'm doing to address this distraction? Does it need to be done now? Is it even urgent, or can it wait until another time? Is it important or necessary to drop what I'm doing to tend to the distraction? Am I using my time wisely? What distractions are stealing my time, keeping me from my prayer time, Bible reading, or walk with the Lord?

Asking questions like these will help you better deal with distractions and will help you single in on the things you may need to change.

Another way to tell that you are becoming distracted is if you start losing focus and even become fidgety. This is usually a real problem for those who are suffering from Spiritual A.D.D. When you start feeling restless and antsy in prayer, for example, try getting up and moving around. Sometimes activity helps bring you back to a place where you can better focus.

If you are dealing with Spiritual A.D.D., you need to be encouraged that there are natural and spiritual solutions you can apply. Sometimes you need to address the devil, who may be trying to distract you. This would be a spiritual solution, and the way to apply it is to do what Jesus taught His disciples regarding the mountain. Tell the enemy he has no place in your life.

At other times, your own spiritual apathy could be contributing to your distraction because you are so busy in natural things. If so, you need to identify what natural things are replacing or affecting your spiritual hunger. Is it an overemphasis on some activity, person, place, or thing? If it is, then you need to make the necessary steps to bring it into order. You do this simply by substituting spiritual things in place of that hindrance. You will be surprised how your hunger will return in your Christian walk. The important thing is to rise up in your heart, your spirit, and decide you aren't going to let any mountain stand in the way of your victory over Spiritual A.D.D. and distractions.

You deal with spiritual distractions in the same way you deal with natural distractions. However, natural distractions can affect you not only in natural things but also in your spiritual life if you are not careful.

If you feel like you have a mountain of Spiritual A.D.D. or distractions that you are facing, here are some considerations that may help you.

Start with writing down a list of things that are wants, needs, and absolutes in your life. When you make this list, be sure that at the top you have time with God as your first priority. Then make note of what things you have to absolutely put first because you can't live without them. Then ask yourself, *What are the things I need to do and give quality attention to?* Finally, ask, *What are some things that I want but that aren't necessarily absolute needs?*

After you have made note of your wants, needs, and absolutes, then make note of your daily and weekly routine and responsibilities by creating a schedule. When you do, consider how you can better prioritize your time. What are things that could be distractions to this schedule? Where are spiritual things listed on this schedule, and how much priority are you giving to them?

This is called *clearing your head*—when you make a list before you go about your time with God. You will find it helpful, and it will limit distractions before and during your time with God. Making a list of the things you need to do, like chores, schedules, work responsibilities, important dates, and other things, will keep you better focused and less distracted. This is one reason why Jesus said not to put your hands to the plow and look back (see Luke 9:62). In other words, stay focused on the spiritual tasks at hand, and don't get distracted.

A good farmer can't plow his field correctly and expect a harvest if he's looking over his shoulder and getting distracted. The result would be crooked rows and precious space and time wasted because of distractions. Also, if you have been suffering from Spiritual A.D.D., do not look back on your frustration or failures, but plow ahead and refuse to focus on the past!

Once you have written out your schedule and determined to prioritize time with God, make sure you have plenty of spiritual things that you are implementing in your schedule. Once you put the schedule to use, it is important to make a note of what specific things start trying to distract you before you spend time with the Lord. Also, it is just as important to do the same thing during your regular times with the Lord—making note of things that try to make you restless and distracted. You need to ask yourself if these distractions are commonly occurring just when you set your heart on spiritual things. If they are, then identify and address them. Always remember the importance of checking your heart attitude when you begin. Are you complaining, yawning, acting bored, going through the routine, or are you really putting your heart excitement in what you are doing?

Don't forget the importance of being well organized and prepared in your times with God to keep your attention focused on the Lord. Consider bringing a list of things to pray, your Bible, a notebook, some worship music, or a Christian book.

Another helpful thing to consider if you are feeling distracted is to check your surroundings. For me, if there is a lot of clutter, my surroundings can be a distraction. You may want to take a look around to see if excess clutter can be removed and to physically clean your surroundings. You will be amazed at how free you feel and how much more you feel like investing in spiritual things when your surroundings are clean and in order. The vital thing is to establish a clean, uncluttered location for time with God, if possible.

If your location is distracting you, perhaps you could choose a different place, one with the least amount of distractions. If it is noise, then try to find a place that is more quiet and peaceful. If that is not an option, consider what things you can do to your current place to make it more peaceful and less of a distraction. If it is the time you are meeting with the Lord that is distracting you (because you are feeling tired or restless), consider praying at another time when you are more alert, or try to get more rest.

If you are still struggling with Spiritual A.D.D. and just can't seem to shake the distractions, consider the possibility of finding an accountability partner to help you stay on course with your spiritual walk or time with God. This is only as good as you want it to be—you have to allow yourself to be accountable.

I hope you were able to find some things from these suggestions that will help you overcome Spiritual A.D.D. I am convinced if you give it some thought and put your heart into identifying and addressing Spiritual A.D.D. and distractions, you will find the joy you are looking for. Are you ready to deal with distractions and remove Spiritual A.D.D. from your spiritual walk? Then I challenge you to step out like Peter, but keep your eyes on the Lord, refusing to become distracted (see Matt. 14:22-32.). Continue to pursue the Lord like Mary, who sat at the feet of the Lord and didn't get caught up in the distractions that affected her sister, Martha (see Luke 10:38-42).

I know that you can do it! All you have to do is step out, keep your eyes on the Lord, and identify and address those distractions. When you do, your spiritual path will be clear, and the future you have desired will be staring you in the face—the life with God that you have dreamed of!

Chapter Five

IT'S NOT WORKING

Simon answered, "Master, we've worked hard all night and haven't caught anything. But because You say so, I will let down the nets" (Luke 5:5 NIV).

When my wife, Brenda, and I were newlyweds, we were living in a small apartment. I will never forget what took place one afternoon while I was praying in the extra bedroom that we had converted into our "ministry office." There was only one problem with that office: We didn't really have any place to minister; so we really couldn't consider it a ministry office, but we did. My wife and I both had a dream and a call to preach that we believed was to take us all over the world. But nobody was calling our phone or requesting for us to minister. They were staying away by the thousands! In fact, it seemed in those beginning days of our ministry together that nothing was working. So we both decided to get jobs outside of our struggling upstart ministry just to make ends meet.

I decided I would pray and study in this little ministry office in our apartment as I always did. I was trying hard in my heart to maintain the faith and belief that we were really called to preach. I had to fight feelings of discouragement, frustration, and disappointment. The harder I tried, the less results it seemed to bring; nothing was working! I continued to pray, all the while not really feeling connected to God. I paced around that little office, praying and pressing in for God to use us and send us to the world. It felt like my prayers were shooting up to the ceiling and falling back down. I took a deep breath and pushed forward, praying some more.

Eventually, I was ready to stop praying and do something else. It felt like things just weren't working, so I thought, *Why continue?* That's when something amazing happened! I decided to stand in front of my brown chair, which I often used to pray and study in, when I thought I saw something move out of the corner of my right eye. I continued standing in prayer, and then I saw it again. With my heart racing I thought, *OK, I am going to just keep praying and ignore it!*

I prayed again and decided to slowly look over my right shoulder. As I did, I saw what appeared to be an angelic figure standing next to me and looking right at me. I knew this was real and not a "pizza" dream because I hadn't eaten any, and, truthfully, we couldn't afford to order any. I didn't know what to do so I folded my hands and bowed my head. The angel folded his hands and bowed his head too! I couldn't believe it! OK, I thought, *I better kneel down in front of my chair.* So I did, and so did that angel! I bowed my head kneeling, and he bowed his head kneeling.

I felt such an awesome reverence for God, so I began to pray, crying out to God for His power and telling Him I wanted to preach around the world. I started calling out places when suddenly it was as if the angel shot out of the room from my chair. Visibly shaken after this event, I sat in my chair, pondering why it had happened. Why was an angel sent, and why did he leave the moment I began praying for open doors around the world?

Over 20 years later, I have come to realize that what I thought wasn't working in those days in fact was! It was working; I just didn't realize it. You see, during the countless hours when my wife and I would pray, calling out to cities and nations specifically (including that day in my "ministry office"), God was listening, and our prayers were working. I know this because my wife and I now have the privilege of ministering all over the world. I believe this is because we kept praying even when it didn't seem like anything was working. It was working; we just had to believe that it was and remain faithful!

It's Not Working

I am sure that I am not the only one who has ever felt like his (or her) prayers weren't being answered or his spiritual walk with God wasn't getting the results he wanted. Have you ever felt that way? Perhaps you are feeling that way now. Maybe it's because you are dealing with Spiritual A.D.D. Whatever you are facing, it is important to remember that even if you can't see the results or what you're doing doesn't seem like its working, you still have to keep pushing forward and be willing to go that extra mile with God, remaining faithful to seek Him. When you aren't seeing the results in your life that you want or when things don't seem like they are working, it is never God's fault. There is always something we need to adjust in our lives in order to bring the blessings and the results we desire.

This reminds me of the story in the Bible when Peter and some fishermen were fishing all night and they caught nothing (see Luke 5:1-11). After their long night of fishing, Jesus arrived on the shore. He saw them cleaning their nets and calling it quits after a night of no results, so the Lord began to teach the people from Peter's boat. After finishing His message, He asked Peter to do something that might have seemed a little pushy.

Jesus asked Peter to do something that would require more work (even though He had seen them clean their nets and probably noticed the lack of fish). He told them to push out into the water farther and try fishing again! *"When He finished teaching, He said to Simon, 'Push out into deep water and let your nets out for a catch'"* (Luke 5:4 MSG).

Does that sound ridiculous? How about pushy? Peter thought so; he informed the Lord that he had already gone fishing in the night and hadn't caught anything. *"Simon answered, 'Master, we've worked hard all night and haven't caught anything'"* (Luke 5:5 NIV). However, Jesus didn't think it was a ridiculous request to ask Peter to keep pushing. In fact, He wasn't at all convinced that it wouldn't work if Peter was willing to try again.

You could say the Lord was pushing him to use his faith and trust Him. He was trying to teach Peter that even though he didn't see any results and it seemed like it wasn't working, he still needed to stretch and try again so the Lord could bless him. I love Jesus' request of Peter, pushing him on to make him try again! Essentially, He was saying, "Peter, pick yourself up and keep doing what you have been doing, but this time do it as I tell you."

Peter was like many who struggle with the symptoms of Spiritual A.D.D. and feel they aren't getting the results they desire in their spiritual lives. He started to make excuses because he felt like he was trying and laboring without the results he wanted. Those who are dealing with Spiritual A.D.D. often pray, worship, read their Bibles, and attend church, yet they feel like things aren't working spiritually for them, so they begin to make excuses. This is due to the symptoms of Spiritual A.D.D. that put more of the focus on what isn't working rather than what is working in their lives.

We need to be encouraged with this example of Peter; what worked for him will work for us. We just have to do what Peter did and let God push us into not giving up but instead trusting in Him. This will enable us to go deeper in our walk with Him and not be afraid to try again.

How did the Lord push Peter? He pushed him by suggesting that he continue to do what he had already done before, even if it didn't seem like it was working. He insisted that Peter should go fishing again by pushing out a little farther into the deep water and trying again. This time, though, he would have to be willing to let Jesus go along with him and do things His way! Jesus wanted Peter to take those extra steps, make that extra decision to pick himself back up, and push forward for results.

This is true for us also, especially if we are experiencing any of the symptoms of Spiritual A.D.D. Rather than taking necessary steps to improve our spiritual walk, we often resort to quitting or making excuses so we don't have to keep trying. What we need to do is what Jesus instructed Peter. We need to press into the things of God, pushing forward, no matter what we face. If we do continue trying, it will bring blessings into our lives. This is what happened to Peter. Once he decided to try again, his net was filled with so many fish that it broke, and he experienced the blessing that he desired. *"And when they had this done, they inclosed a great multitude of fishes: and their net brake"* (Luke 5:6).

Imagine the surprised look on those fishermen after they saw the results! Their nets broke in an amazing way. In fact, I bet after this happened, Peter didn't mind that the Lord had pushed him to try fishing again. Notice that once Peter obeyed and tried again, a breakthrough came. It was only after he was willing to push himself to go farther and keep trying that it worked. Peter had to be willing to do things the way Jesus instructed him in order to get the results he wanted. In the same way we have be willing to launch out, go deeper, and press in a little harder to get those desired results.

Jesus had to do this also. He had to push Himself in order to achieve His desired results. He did this to keep Himself connected to God and not subject to the incredible amount of pressure that He was feeling. *"And going a little farther, He fell on the ground and kept praying that if it were possible the [fatal] hour might pass from Him"* (Mark 14:35 AMP).

SPIRITUAL A.D.D.

In this verse, the Lord went a little farther and kept praying. He didn't give up in the midst of pressure; rather He kept pressing! He didn't stop seeking His Heavenly Father, no matter how He was feeling. This same principle is key for anyone suffering from Spiritual A.D.D.

Don't give up in your pursuit of God, especially if you are feeling like your spiritual life isn't working. You have to push yourself like Peter did and keep rowing and rowing until you reach that place where you receive your breakthrough! You do this simply by continuing to push forward and pray, going further little by little until you reach that place where the symptoms of Spiritual A.D.D. aren't dictating your spiritual life. You just have to be willing, like Jesus was that night in the Garden of Gethsemane, to take those little steps of obedience. It will work if you don't quit! God is working for you, and He is on your side. You just need to remember to stay faithful to do your part in prayer, righteousness, and the continual pursuit of the things of God. Then watch as God is faithful to show up and give you the results you have been wanting.

This is what I came to realize that day in my prayer time when I saw that angel. I did my part, and God was showing me that He was doing His. He was there to help me, and it was working! I just needed to keep seeking God, keep reading my Bible, and remain faithful in my spiritual life to Him.

Are you willing to push yourself to get the results you desire with the Lord? Do you want to have success in your spiritual life, like Peter wanted that day in his fishing? If so, I want to encourage you go a little further, to do what Jesus suggested to Peter and try again! Are you ready to give it another try? Let's launch out together and keep taking those little steps.

Practical Steps Little by Little

Perhaps you are wondering what kind of little steps to make to defeat Spiritual A.D.D. and see better results in your spiritual life. One of the first steps could be making a determined decision to launch out or push yourself in your spiritual walk. A second step is to do what Peter finally did. Think about it for a moment. He had to be willing to work for it in order to get the results he wanted. It required him to row little by little, going farther with each rowing motion. He had to keep making the decision to go deeper. He had to be obedient, willing to work at it again. He had to be determined and consistent if he wanted to see results.

> *Therefore, brethren, be all the more diligent to make certain about His calling and choosing you; for as long as you practice these things, you will never stumble* (2 Peter 1:10 NASB).

— 141 —

SPIRITUAL A.D.D.

We have to be diligent about the things of God and what He has asked us to do for Him. In the same way, when you decide that Spiritual A.D.D. isn't going to hinder you anymore, you will have to push yourself, being diligent to take small steps to overcome it. Then you will see amazing blessing and breakthroughs in your spiritual life like Peter did that night.

It isn't usually the big steps that lead to the breaking of Spiritual A.D.D. from us but rather the consistent, little-by-little steps that cause us to overcome. The Bible says our spiritual growth occurs step by step, little by little with consistency. *"For precept must be upon precept, precept upon precept; line upon line, line upon line; here a little, and there a little"* (Isa. 28:10). The consistent little choices will cause things to work in our spiritual lives again—like reading the Bible again for a few minutes or getting back to being consistent in church attendance. Maybe that small step is just planning a little time with God each day and gradually increasing its duration.

It is important to take small, decisive steps when dealing with overcoming Spiritual A.D.D. because if we try to take too big of steps at first, we can become frustrated if change doesn't seem to be happening immediately. Change is often a process that requires heart, dedication, commitment, and consistency. It is the little-by-little daily choices to push ourselves to give God our best, not the giant steps that don't last, that will get us the results we are seeking.

Remember, Jesus took that small push forward when He prayed in the Garden of Gethsemane. We have to be determined like He was and press forward. This determination and pushing forward kept Jesus from getting off course and becoming affected by the enormous pressure and spiritual attack coming against Him. Through it all, He pushed and pressed forward, continuing to seek His Heavenly Father.

We have to be determined just like that, and each time we feel the pressure to quit, we need to rise up and press forward in our spiritual lives by pushing ourselves and setting necessary goals to go a little further each time. When we do, it will help us to not feel bound or struggle with Spiritual A.D.D. The important thing is to never forget that Jesus went forward a little at a time and then to consider how far He got! Look at the results! Fighting Spiritual A.D.D. is a process that requires consistent, little-by-little steps to overcome.

We can take little practical steps to help us launch out a little further in our walk with God. In Chapter 14 of Mark, we find some practical tools we can use when we feel that our spiritual lives aren't working as we'd like, or we are suffering from Spiritual A.D.D. Let's look at a simple pattern of the events in Jesus' life before and during His prayer in the Garden of Gethsemane. I will highlight key words and events that we can easily apply as principles in our lives as we desire to push forward and see results. They are small steps that can lead to big results in our spiritual lives with God!

Mark 14:17-37

1. **Set a Time**—*"And in the evening He cometh with the twelve"* (Mark 14:17). Morning is usually best, but maybe there is a time that works better with your schedule. The key is to "set" a time and stay consistent.

2. **Seek God's Kingdom First**—*"...He cometh with the twelve"* (Mark 14:17). The number 12 is a prophetic number that symbolizes God's Kingdom (His way of doing things). When we seek and put God's Kingdom first, we will see results (see Matt. 6:33).

3. **Take Communion Often**—(see Mark 14:22-25). We can take communion as often as we need to (see 1 Cor. 11:25).

    *   Claim the five blessings of the bread. Five things happened when Jesus broke bread with His disciples after the Resurrection (see Luke 24:31-32): 1) "their eyes were opened"—they received revelation knowledge; 2) "they knew Him"; 3) their "heart burn[ed] within them"; 4) "He talked with us"—they heard God's voice; 5) "He

opened us the Scriptures." As believers, we can claim these five things also.

- Claim the seven blessings of the blood—power, riches, wisdom, strength, honor, glory, and blessing (see Rev. 5:12). Jesus received these seven blessings as the Lamb of God who was slain, and they are now given and available to us as joint heirs in Him.

4. **Remember to Worship**—*"And when they had sung an hymn, they went out into the mount of Olives"* (Mark 14:26). Make worship a part of your life as Ephesians 5:18-20 encourages.

5. **Keep Your Heart Right**—*"And Jesus saith unto them, All ye shall be offended because of Me this night..."* (Mark 14:27). Live a repentant and forgiving life (see Mark 11:25). It is important not to get offended or have unforgiveness in our hearts, which can hinder our prayers. Therefore, we must keep our hearts right by staying in love, walking pure, and avoiding offenses and unforgiveness.

6. **Set a Place**—*"And they came to a place which was named Gethsemane..."* (Mark 14:32). Establish a regular place to meet with God.

7. **Be Fervent**—Jesus prayed in a garden called Gethsemane, which means *"oil press"* in the Greek.[1] This reveals the importance of pressing in with your heart in prayer for the power of God to manifest. The key is to find a place where you can fervently press into God's presence.

8. **Pray With Others**—*"...Sit ye here, while I shall pray. And He taketh with Him Peter and James and John, and began to be sore amazed, and to be very heavy"* (Mark 14:32-33). Praying with others is a great way to defeat Spiritual A.D.D.

9. **Set Prayer Goals**—*"And He went forward a little, and fell on the ground, and prayed..."* (Mark 14:35). Continue to set goals, going further each time in your pursuit of the Lord.

10. **Resist Falling Asleep**—*"And He cometh, and findeth them sleeping, and saith unto Peter, Simon, sleepest thou? couldest not thou watch one hour?"* (Mark 14:37).

11. **Build Up to an Hour**—*"...couldest not thou watch one hour?"* (Mark 14:37). Discipline yourself by trying to establish a consistent hour of devotions with the Lord. Do your

best to avoid a fast-food, drive-through mentality of seeking God where you are in and out with your order within five minutes.

These are little steps you can take to better push yourself to launch out in the deeper things of God. Taking note of them will also help you better prepare yourself to be with God, getting the results that you desire.

How Prepared Are You?

Another little, but effective, way to push ourselves in our spiritual lives so that we can start seeing the results we desire, is to come prepared, stay prepared, and refuse to become discouraged and give up. This just requires a small step of taking a moment and becoming better prepared.

When we aren't prepared and organized, our spiritual lives often suffer, especially our devotional lives. This is because of the tendency to approach our devotions haphazardly and not well prepared. In other words, if we handle our time carelessly, we may drag ourselves into our prayer time not expecting results. When this happens, we can start wishing to do something else rather than spending time doing spiritual things. This can result in boredom and feeling like we are just going through the motions. We can start feeling like it's just not working, which affects our spiritual attitudes.

SPIRITUAL A.D.D.

This is how Spiritual A.D.D. works. It is meant to get us to stay in neutral, never progressing in our spiritual lives; it can even get us going in reverse, causing us to back up spiritually and eventually quit—at least on the inside. When this starts to happen, we need to take some small steps to get things working again. We can accomplish this by being determined to push ourselves to keep trying in our spiritual lives, regardless of the obstacles before us. We do this by making a decision to take those small steps that will further launch our spiritual lives in the right direction so we can get the results we are seeking.

Here are some simple and helpful things we can do that will help us get those results. They will help us to prepare and recharge, or jump start, our spiritual lives.

Take a moment to see how prepared you are. Whenever you decide you are going to go deeper, like Peter did, I suggest you start coming prepared to your time with God so you can get better results. The more prepared, expectant, and hungry you are, the easier it is to defeat Spiritual A.D.D. God knew the importance of this simple step in order to have maximum results. He told Moses in the Bible to make sure the people were prepared to meet with Him.

> *The LORD also said to Moses, "Go to the people and consecrate them today and tomorrow, and let them wash their garments; and let them be ready for the*

third day, for on the third day the Lord will come down on Mount Sinai in the sight of all the people (Exodus 19:10-11 NASB).

This was in order to help them get the maximum benefits of their time with God by being well prepared before meeting with Him.

Another example of this can be found in the Bible regarding the Shunammite woman (see 2 Kings 4:9-10). She wanted to prepare a room for the prophet Elisha to meet with God. He visited frequently, but she wanted to increase his ability to have special times with God. She did this by preparing things in a room for him. She took a determined approach that included some practical items to help him prepare to meet with the Lord. These same things can help us launch our spiritual lives forward. When we prepare ourselves, we can kick Spiritual A.D.D. goodbye!

Let's take a look at the things we need to have and do in our prayer rooms that will help us get results.

2 Kings 4:9-10

- **A Chamber** (a place to pray, your prayer closet or place of prayer)—This is to help you establish your set place of prayer and meeting with God.

- **A Candlestick** (the right physical atmosphere)—Having the proper lighting helps to set the atmosphere that gets the best results you are seeking, helping you to focus better. If you are struggling with falling asleep, try turning on a light!

- **A Bed** (the place to meditate, listen, and rest before God)—This speaks of having somewhere that is comfortable to meditate on God and rest, being quiet before Him. This is so you can hear God's voice and let Him minister to you as well!

- **A Stool** (the best posture)—This is where you can sit, pray, and study to get the best results. If you are struggling to stay awake, for example, try a different posture, like pacing.

- **A Table** (the right material to be fed spiritually)—The table speaks of having your Bible and other biblical material with you in your devotions. It speaks of being organized and prepared in your reading and studying of the Word of God. The table is the place where you can be prepared to feed on God's Word, study, and enjoy God's presence.

- **A Bed and Table** (the balance of rest and spiritual labor)—The bed and the table are different items; however, both are necessary for overcoming Spiritual A.D.D. The table is for work and feeding, while the bed is for rest. Both of these are important in your spiritual life.

As we can see, these items were necessary to aid Elisha in his spiritual life. They will work for us also and will better prepare us when we spend time with God.

Take a moment to consider these items in your life and even determine what you need to do to better prepare yourself to be with God. This is important because you may not actually be dealing with Spiritual A.D.D. symptoms but rather with the lack of preparation and organization. If you will become better prepared and purposeful, it will greatly increase your spiritual results and keep you from feeling like your spiritual life isn't working.

The Lord and Pity Parties

When we are battling Spiritual A.D.D. and feeling as though things are not working as we desire, the worst thing we can do is to start feeling sorry for ourselves and begin to get negative. These struggles can affect each person differently, but we can all agree on the importance of keeping our faith and trust in the Lord. We have to guard our hearts against unbelief and developing a mindset of, "It won't work so, why should I try anymore?" If this is our mindset, it can lead to a pity party.

The Lord loves parties, except those that indulge in sinful practices or the ones full of feeling sorry for ourselves and making up excuses. Those are called pity parties. This doesn't imply that He doesn't care or isn't touched by our problems or that we aren't allowed to show emotion. We know the Lord is compassionate, loving, longsuffering, and full of mercy. However, He won't be manipulated by our emotions or compelled to step in just because we are offended or feeling sorry for ourselves. This may sound kind of harsh, but it's the truth. We will examine a few examples of pity parties in Scripture.

Lazarus

In one example, Jesus had a friend named Lazarus who was very sick and later died. The news traveled back to Jesus, who, after a few days of waiting, went to raise Lazarus from the dead. This did not go over well with those who felt He should have come earlier to prevent Lazarus' death. Jesus arrived in Bethany, the place where Lazarus was buried, knowing that He would raise him from the dead, and encountered a party scene— not one of celebration but of grief, sorrow, and blaming Him. This pity party scene was so bad that both of Lazarus' sisters, Mary and Martha, tried to blame Jesus for their brother's death. *"Then said Martha unto Jesus,*

Lord, if Thou hadst been here, my brother had not died" (John 11:21). We can see that Martha was blaming Jesus while her sister Mary stayed in her house having a pity party. *"Then Martha, as soon as she heard that Jesus was coming, went and met Him: but Mary sat still in the house"* (John 11:20). Mary later blamed Jesus just like her sister.

> *Then when Mary was come where Jesus was, and saw Him, she fell down at His feet, saying unto Him, Lord, if Thou hadst been here, my brother had not died* (John 11:32).

It is important to note that Jesus was friends with this family, yet He purposely didn't join their weeping, sorrow, and display of unbelief. You might be saying, "Wait a minute, doesn't the Bible say that Jesus wept in this same story?" That's right; Jesus did weep in this story. *"Jesus wept"* (John 11:35). However, the better question to ask is, "Why did He weep?" Was it to join their pity party of blame, unbelief, and feeling sorry? No, He wept in regard to their display of unbelief and their commotion. *"When Jesus therefore saw her weeping, and the Jews also weeping which came with her, He groaned in the spirit, and was troubled"* (John 11:33).

Jesus saw them weeping, and He was troubled. This is not to imply that He was angry at their weeping; He was angry at why they were weeping. In other words, He saw something He didn't like in the way they were weeping and carrying on; He became troubled and groaned in His spirit about it. This doesn't sound like He was on board with their pity party, does it? What does it mean to be troubled and to groan in the spirit? What is the difference between Jesus who "wept" and the people who were "weeping"? To better understand the difference and why Jesus was troubled and groaned about it, we have to look more closely at the meaning of these words—*groaned, trouble, wept,* and *weeping.*

Groaned in spirit is translated from the Greek word *embrimaomai.* It means to be moved with anger; to admonish sternly; to snort with the notion of coercion, springing out of displeasure, anger, indignation, antagonism; to express indignant displeasure with someone; and to charge sternly. It also means to snort like an angry horse, literally to "snort (roar) with rage," which expresses strong indignation, i.e. deep feeling that is moved to sternly admonish.[2]

Troubled is from the Greek word *tarassó.* It means to agitate back and forth, shake to and fro, trouble, and agitate, causing inner perplexity and emotional agitation from getting too stirred up inside and upset.[3]

Wept comes from the Greek word *dakrýō.*[4] This is also from the Greek word *dákry.* It means a teardrop or to properly shed quiet actual tears, to weep silently with tears.[5]

Weeping is the Greek word *klaiō*.[6] This means to properly weep aloud, expressing uncontainable, audible grief, audible weeping, and to sob, i.e. wail aloud. It is different from the word wept (*dakruo*), which, as we have seen, means to cry silently.

Do you see the difference? Jesus wept (verse 35) in control of His emotions and spirit, shedding quiet actual tears, while the other people were weeping loud and fleshly tears (verse 33). Jesus' "teardrop" and His properly shedding quiet tears, according to the definition, certainly implies the Lord's heart and how He is touched with the feeling of our infirmities. Yet, what troubled Him, causing Him to agitate back and forth and be stirred up inside, like the definition says, was that the people were emotional and out of control, creating a scene—and not one of believing Him to raise Lazarus but of blame and unbelief! In other words, they were having a pity party that Jesus didn't join. There is a difference between their weeping and moaning and the kind of mourning due to the loss of a loved one. Mourning is legitimate feeling of grief, but moaning is different—a complaining and "poor ole me" attitude on display.

Some of these people weren't mourning; instead they were moaning and carrying on, hoping they could move Jesus to intervene because nothing they did worked! Jesus responded by showing His anger and disapproval of their commotion (based on the definitions of *groan* and *trouble*). We can see from these definitions that Jesus was angry, moving His head back and forth like an angry horse snorting in defiance! Studying these words makes it very apparent that He didn't approve of their display and He didn't join their pity party!

Jesus didn't weep in the same manner of those He saw weeping. Instead, He was groaning in His spirit and not in His flesh or emotions, like the others who were weeping. He was groaning against the powers of darkness and the fleshly acts of the people who were carrying on in a pity party of self-pity, blame, offense, and out-of-control emotion.

Does the Lord feel any different today when we carry on the same way as these people? At some point we have to quit feeling sorry for ourselves, complaining, murmuring, and getting upset if our spiritual lives aren't working. If we are dealing with Spiritual A.D.D., we need to not complain or carry on in a fleshly way but rather be willing to push ourselves to overcome it the right way. In fact, God takes note of our constant complaining, murmuring, and feeling sorry for ourselves. You may have heard some people say, "God keeps the score." And they are right—He does! God keeps count (or score) of how many times we murmur and complain!

Because all those men which have seen My glory, and My miracles, which I did in Egypt and in the

> *wilderness, and have tempted Me now these **ten***
> ***times**, and have not hearkened to My voice* (Numbers 14:22).

The reason the Lord was counting was because the Israelites' words and attitude were wrong. They were having a pity party against Moses and the Lord. Whether we are dealing with Spiritual A.D.D. or not, we still have to watch our words and attitudes so we don't hinder God's blessings in our lives.

Cain

Another example in Scripture of the Lord not attending a pity party is when Cain decided he was going to have one because he offered to God an offering that was unacceptable in the Lord's sight.

> *And Abel brought of the firstborn of his flock and of the fat portions. And the Lord had respect and regard for Abel and for his offering, but for Cain and his offering He had no respect or regard. So Cain was exceedingly angry and indignant, and he looked sad and depressed* (Genesis 4:4-5 AMP).

His brother Abel gave his best by offering to God the first of what he had, but this wasn't the case with Cain. He developed a bad attitude with the Lord and began to feel sorry for himself. He became angry, indignant, sad, and depressed. He started his pity party and had a tantrum because he hadn't given the Lord his best!

However, the Lord wasn't going to join his pity party, so He asked why he was acting all sad and depressed. *"God spoke to Cain: 'Why this tantrum? Why the sulking?...'"* (Gen. 4:6 MSG). He even told him that he needed to adjust, by pushing himself to do what was right. *"If you do what is right, will you not be accepted? But if you do not do what is right, sin is crouching at your door..."* (Gen. 4:7 NIV).

It sounds a lot like what we read about Peter being asked by the Lord to step out and try again. Cain would have had to decide not to have a pity party and to try again, by doing what was right, if he was to receive the desired blessings.

Spiritual A.D.D. is meant to discourage us and keep us from getting the results we want. It's intended to get us to feel sorry for ourselves. The effects of Spiritual A.D.D. are meant to convince us that our time with God or our spiritual lives aren't having any real benefit. When this happens, we can really get down on ourselves and end up not giving our best to God, like Cain. Sometimes we can even condemn ourselves and feel like failures before the Lord. If we are not careful, we can even think that God doesn't understand and decide that we are going to have a pity party. We can start to feel sorry for ourselves and develop an unhealthy attitude that affects our spiritual outlook.

Unfortunately, the kind of behavior that Cain displayed is common among some church folk today and those who take Spiritual A.D.D. to the extreme. People often come into church or walk around in their spiritual lives moody, sad, and depressed—and everyone knows they are having another bad day like Cain did. Sometimes people are afraid to ask such people how they are doing for fear of receiving a life-long list of negative things, which most of the time aren't really that bad or are blown out of proportion.

This is not to suggest that some people don't legitimately have situations where they need someone to understand and care. However, if asked whether they are praying, those same people will often respond with, "Oh, yes, I spend lots of time reading my Bible and in the presence of the Lord praying." I have just one problem with this: The Bible says that in the presence of the Lord there is much joy (see Ps. 16:11). Thus, it is not hard to conclude that these people probably aren't really praying and pursuing God as hard and as often as they imply; if they were, the fruit of it would be joy, not depression and pity parties.

The sun isn't going to stop for this kind of people or for our pity parties. The only time the sun stopped still was in the days of Joshua (see Josh. 10:12-14—the sun stood still and the moon stayed). It didn't stop because God felt sorry for poor old Joshua, who was in a major battle in his life. Joshua got the Lord's intervention because he wouldn't have a pity party. Instead, he got up, refused to quit, and went into battle with the power of God on his side! He refused to have a pity party and kept trying until he won!

Why Make This "Ado"?

When dealing with Spiritual A.D.D., it is not always easy to be like Joshua and feel like rising up and fighting for what belongs to us. As we have seen, when it doesn't look like things are working in our spiritual lives, we can start to feel sorry for ourselves if we are not careful, and begin to have a pity party. It then becomes easier to create a scene or resort to what Jesus called "making an ado." *"...He saith unto them, Why make ye this ado, and weep?..."* (Mark 5:39).

"Making an ado" is kind of like a pity party, but it is more along the lines of overreacting, complaining, and responding in uncontrolled emotion and fear. Before we get to the scriptural example, let me share a story from my life that gives a clear picture of "making an ado."

I crawled into my prayer time literally feeling the weight of the things that had to get done in the ministry. I felt like Spiritual A.D.D. was trying to knock at the door of my prayer room. In addition, spiritual attacks were coming against some of my relatives and family. I thought, *I don't need this, God,* and I started to mumble and complain, full of unbelief. I was angry that things weren't working in my life as I thought they should be. I was speaking wrong, praying wrong, and exhibiting a bad attitude with the Lord. This went on for some time, and the longer I exhibited this and prayed this way, somehow I knew God wasn't impressed or getting on my spiritual bandwagon.

I am not saying we can't or shouldn't be honest with God or that He isn't interested in helping us. Yet, God is moved by faith, so He was not moved by my unbelief, complaining, murmuring, and feeling-sorry-for-myself attitude.

> *But without faith it is impossible to please Him: for he that cometh to God must believe that He is, and that He is a rewarder of them that diligently seek Him* (Hebrews 11:6).

I continued in my state of defeat and even began to plan my own spiritual pity party when the Lord finally spoke to me to stop. I laugh today at what He said, especially when He again quoted from the King James Version of the Bible! I have already told how He had spoken this way to me another time, and I won't be surprised if He does so to me again. God's sense of humor with me amazes me. After all, He is the source of all joy and laughter; He created it.

He spoke that wonderful phrase—that I didn't want to hear. He said, "Hank, why are you making this ado?"

SPIRITUAL A.D.D.

I knew the Lord was quoting from this verse we have been looking at in Mark chapter 5, when Jairus' daughter had died and people were creating a very loud, emotional scene. *"And when He was come in, He saith unto them, Why make ye this ado, and weep?..."* (Mark 5:39). I personally haven't met anyone who uses the word *ado*. Yet, I knew what the Lord was referring to with me and what it meant in modern terminology. Today we might say to someone who's making an ado, "Why are you freaking out or getting all worked up?"

This is exactly what I was doing! I was carrying on with a bad attitude, weariness, and a real mentality of defeat. I didn't think that things were working in my life, and I wanted to have an attitude about it. This is the danger when we feel like we are dealing with the symptoms of Spiritual A.D.D. We can start to resort to making an ado! Sometimes we think carrying on or walking around in a spiritual stupor will somehow get God's attention or cause the problem to just go away on its own.

However, I have learned that we have to do what Jesus did that day at Jairus' house. He had to confront the ado. He did this by making all the people leave who were making a loud scene of crying and unbelief. They were laughing at Jesus in a way that was belittling Him and mocking Him. They were convinced that raising this girl from the dead wouldn't work and He was just wasting His time. However, the Lord wouldn't let it distract Him from having a miracle breakthrough.

> *And they laughed Him to scorn. But when He had put them all out, He taketh the father and the mother of the damsel, and them that were with Him, and entereth in where the damsel was lying* (Mark 5:40).

The Lord responded to this display of ado in the same way we need to treat Spiritual A.D.D. He confronted it, didn't tolerate it, and put it out of the house. This is exactly what we need to do! We can't just ignore it, complain about it, or get all emotional. We have to decide today to rise up and see ourselves enjoying spiritual lives that are full of spiritual vitality and results. We need to do what Jesus did with those who are making ado; He showed them the door to leave. We need to be determined that Spiritual A.D.D. has to go from our lives! When we do, we will see our spiritual lives come to life like Jairus' daughter! We have to be willing to work for it and push ourselves to go deeper, just like Peter.

If you will refuse to quit, like Jesus, and press on to go further in your walk with God until you see results, you will find what you have been seeking. I encourage you to rise up, try again, and say, "No pity parties here!" I encourage you to keep resisting the temptation to quit or feel sorry for yourself. If you are struggling with Spiritual A.D.D., establish a "no ado" policy! If you do, I am certain that your prayer life will work, and your spiritual life will be reenergized.

Are you ready to push yourself a little, step by step, until you see your breakthrough? Then I encourage you to get back in your boat like Peter did, prepare yourself, and launch out into the deep. Push yourself and resist Spiritual A.D.D., which wants to keep you in neutral or self-pity. Rise up and start pushing forward! You will be surprisingly blessed if you do. You will experience the results Peter did that day when he pushed himself to try again. When he did, to his surprise, blessing and abundant breakthroughs were waiting! He just needed to put his heart and effort behind what Jesus wanted. It will work again! It is working! Ready? Start launching forward into the deep! You will be surprised at the outcome, and you will be glad you did!

Endnotes

1. James Strong, *The New Strong's Exhaustive Concordance of the Bible* (Nashville, TN: Thomas Nelson, 1991), Greek #1068.

2. *Ibid.*, Greek #1690.

3. *Ibid.*, Greek #5015.

4. *Ibid.*, Greek #1145.

5. *Ibid.*, Greek #1144.

6. *Ibid.*, Greek #2799.

Chapter Six

JOY AGAIN IN MY SALVATION

Yet I will rejoice in the LORD, I will joy in the God of my salvation (Habakkuk 3:18).

I will never forget the day I got a phone call from someone who wanted to visit me. Brenda and I had just returned from a ministry trip, and we were not really in the mood for company. Yet, this person kept insisting, so I hesitantly agreed. A few hours later, I was glad I had. He had come to visit us because he had been impressed by the Lord to give us a new car! I remember looking at his hand, holding car keys, with my mouth opened in surprise by what he said to me. "Go ahead. This is yours, Hank and Brenda. These are the keys to a brand-new car. The Lord told me to give this to you, and you are to trade it in and get the one you want," he said, as he handed us the keys.

We were so grateful to the Lord because we had believed for a new car. This was especially a blessing because many of the vehicles we had owned before this were nothing to speak of. We had a car that caught fire when running too long and cars that had more rust on them than paint. We had never owned a new one at that point in our marriage. So we did exactly as he said and traded that new car in for a minivan, which is what we had believed for.

I must admit, during this time I was wrestling with feelings of guilt, like I didn't deserve this blessing. It wasn't until we were on the way to the auto dealership in a different city to trade the new car in that the Lord gave me a vision of the new van we were to buy. I remember how clear the vision was. The Lord showed me the color of this new van—green on the exterior with a camel brown interior—sitting on the showroom floor. I was surprised by this picture and shared it with Brenda. The vision was interesting to both of us because neither one of us had ever discussed wanting a green van with a camel interior. In fact, green was one of our least likely colors to consider!

But when we pulled up to the dealership, we saw the green van the Lord had showed me sitting right in the middle of the showroom floor, looking out the window at us. It was as if it was staring at us, waving, with our name on it! We were super excited and thankful to the Lord as we traded in the new car we had been blessed with and bought the van that He had graciously provided. My wife and I were so happy as we drove it off the car lot. It was fully loaded and fully paid for. It couldn't get any better than that!

As I said, we had never, ever had a vehicle this nice in the few years we had been married. We told everyone—I mean everyone, everywhere—that the Lord had given us this van. It was practically our newborn, and we were proud parents! Whether they cared or wanted to hear it, we told everyone. It was our testimony, and we were sticking to it. We even bought a Jesus logo for the back. We were dedicated to letting the whole world know of our blessing. We were so filled with joy!

But there was one little problem. Over time, that van didn't behave itself. Its gas tank went out; its transmission had to be replaced; an antifreeze leak stained the carpet; there were electrical problems; and the air conditioning went out. Oh my! We drove it for 13 years, and it was a blessing despite the few setbacks. Ultimately, I had to get rid of it because of a very loud—I mean very loud—noise coming from the engine! People could hear us coming for miles and turned their heads to look at our noisy van. It got so bad my kids begged me to drop them off miles from their school; they would rather walk than have their friends see them riding in this van.

It's quite a story, but the point I want to make is in regard to our salvation experiences. Most of us start off joyful and excited, just like Brenda and I were with the brand-new van. Life is so sweet; it couldn't get any better. In fact, we tell everyone we meet what God has done for us. But then (oh, that dreaded word) we start having problems, like we had with this van. Then we start getting angry, even embarrassed, that we have such a thing called salvation. In our spiritual lives, it's called *neglecting our salvation*.

Neglecting Our Salvation

My experience with the new van is often how we treat our salvation experience with Jesus. We can start to neglect it because we start losing the new joy, excitement, and appreciation that we first had when we gave our hearts to the Lord. We can tend to lose interest with God and spiritual things if we are not careful. We also neglect our salvation if we begin to not appreciate our relationship with God when it doesn't "feel" like or "look" like it once did. It's the same as with my van when it made that awful noise. We stop telling people about God. The excitement and joy wears off because things start going wrong. We then become too embarrassed to tell anyone that we love God. The key is, no matter what, we can't allow Spiritual A.D.D. to cause us to lose our joy, that precious joy of our salvation.

This is exactly what Habakkuk tells us—*No matter what, keep your joy!* Look at what was happening that could have made Israel lose their joy and stop praising God.

> *Even though the fig trees have no blossoms, and there are no grapes on the vines; even though the olive crop fails, and the fields lie empty and barren; even though the flocks die in the fields, and the cattle barns are empty* (Habakkuk 3:17 NLT).

Do the things that happened in this verse sound familiar? In other words, maybe we are not getting spiritually fed, or things are really going badly in our lives, and we are facing many difficulties. We have all faced difficulties from time to time and know what it is like to suffer and have to do without. Yet, in all of these things, we need to guard against getting down and depressed! The next verse tells us what we should do if we are facing problems and things seem to be failing around us. *"Yet I will rejoice in the LORD! I will be joyful in the God of my salvation!"* (Hab. 3:18 NLT).

This verse is telling us that we should keep our joy no matter what. This means that if we want to enjoy our Christian life, it can't be based on feelings alone. There will be plenty of things in this life that will to try to get us down. This verse reminds us that if everything else fails in life, we still have the joy of our salvation in the Lord. God has it under control. We can trust Him.

SPIRITUAL A.D.D.

When we start neglecting our salvation, this can result in the loss of the joy and the excitement of being a Christian. Spiritual A.D.D. can contribute to neglect of our salvation through constant procrastination, distractions, struggling to pay attention, restlessness, and tiredness, to name a few. If over time Spiritual A.D.D. goes undetected or is not dealt with, it causes us to neglect the joy that is available in a healthy walk with God.

When Spiritual A.D.D. affects us, especially in the form of neglect, we start feeling less like praying or even reading our Bibles. Often when we do choose to invest time in spiritual things it can seem boring and unfulfilling. This is usually because we are neglecting something in our walk with God. The word *neglect* means to pay little or no attention to; to fail to heed; to disregard; to fail to care for or attend to properly, through carelessness or oversight; to leave undone or unattended to. These definitions reveal many ways that neglect works to try to steal the joy that is in our salvation with God.

I am not saying that people who neglect their salvation aren't going to Heaven. We all have to work out our own salvation, as the Scripture says, with fear and trembling (see Phil. 2:12). What I am referring to is losing the joy that we had when we first became Christians or losing the joy of serving God. In fact, we are told in Scripture not to neglect so great a salvation: *"How shall we escape, if we neglect so great salvation..."* (Heb. 2:3).

I want you to think for a minute if neglect may be affecting the joy of your salvation. Is there anything in your spiritual life that you know you should be doing that you're not? Are you doing anything that you need to adjust, something that is causing you to neglect your spiritual life?

It's different for all of us. Yet, there are usually obvious signs that indicate if we are starting to lose the joy of our salvation. They are indicators that Spiritual A.D.D. is affecting our Christian walk. One of the first indications is when we hardly read the Word of God and it doesn't hold our interest. If that is the case, we need to do what David said in the Bible. *"I will delight myself in Thy statutes: I will not forget Thy word"* (Ps. 119:16). The Word of God is to be a joy in our lives and not something that we should neglect. The more we feed on it, the more joy and success we will have in our lives.

> *Thy words were found, and I did eat them; and Thy*
> *word was unto me the joy and rejoicing of mine heart:*
> *for I am called by Thy name, O LORD God of hosts*
> (Jeremiah 15:16).

Another way to gauge if we are neglecting our salvation is if we start developing a habitual routine of neglecting our prayer lives or approaching our time with God halfheartedly. This is why we must keep a tight grip on our schedule with God and be on alert for distractions. Something else that becomes apparent when we are losing the joy of our salvation is when we neglect telling others about the Lord. We seldom tell others about Him as it becomes less of a thought or priority.

When these things are common occurrences in our lives, it is apparent that we are starting to lose the joy of our salvation. This means that Spiritual A.D.D. is taking hold of our spiritual lives through the lack of Bible reading, interest in spiritual things, prayer, and soul winning, to name a few. Yet, there is still another dangerous sign that we are losing the joy of our salvation. It is the neglect of our spiritual walk or testimony. This means we seldom invest in the growth of our spiritual walk, and most people wouldn't recognize that we are Christians. This could be because we don't exhibit the fruit of a true follower of Jesus, according to the Bible. This is why we need to seriously examine our lives as to whether we are being influenced by the symptoms of Spiritual A.D.D. Are they causing us to neglect our salvation? Have we lost that very important joy in serving God?

Get Things Flowing Again

If we want to restore the joy in our salvation and avoid spiritual neglect, then we need to see if there is anything in our lives hindering the flow of God. Sometimes we have to prime our spiritual lives like an old water pump on a farmstead. We have to keep pumping the handle until the water flows. Sometimes, if that pump hasn't been used in a while, it will take extra work and some time to get things flowing again. It is the same way when we neglect our salvation and feel like we are losing the joy in our salvation. It may take a while to get things flowing again, but we need to keep working at it until we do. God is calling out to our hearts, wanting to be involved in every facet of our lives. This is what the Scripture means when it says that the deep calls unto the deep. *"Deep calleth unto deep at the noise of Thy waterspouts: all Thy waves and Thy billows are gone over me"* (Ps. 42:7).

This means God's Spirit, who lives in our hearts if we are saved, longs to fellowship with us. God is always calling out to our hearts. God has put everything we need to make it in this life inside of our hearts. When we are Christians, we have the Lord in us, who is the hope of glory (see Col. 1:27). This means we also then have joy already inside of us; it is not something that we are necessarily trying to obtain. We can do certain things to develop and deepen our relationship with the Lord. They are simple things, really, that will get things flowing again and bring back the joy that seems to be missing in our salvation. They are important steps that will really revitalize our walk with God.

One way to begin to do this is what I refer to as "drawing from the wells of our salvation." When we realize God has provided everything we need inside our hearts to enjoy our Christian walk, then it is not difficult to draw it out. Once we know it is just waiting to be drawn out of our hearts or the well of our salvation, like water from a well or a farm pump, we just need to learn how to draw it out. How do we do that? First, we need to understand that our hearts or spirits are like a well of salvation that Jesus said springs up to everlasting life.

> *But whosoever drinketh of the water that I shall give him shall never thirst; but the water that I shall give him shall be in him a well of water springing up into everlasting life* (John 4:14).

Sometimes this spiritual well can get stopped up with so many things in this life, including Spiritual A.D.D. Spiritual A.D.D. certainly contributes to hindering the flow of God in our lives. The well of our hearts is often like that old water pump on a farmstead. If left unattended or unused for a while, it may get rusty or even clogged. We have to literally keep pumping and pumping the handle until clear water begins to flow again. It might seem like we are wasting our time or never getting to that clear place when we are working the handle to get the pump working. This is because at first it might not look like any water is going to flow out of the pump. Sometimes, to our surprise, we may get some dirt, cobwebs, and even some old crusty rust when we first start pumping the handle.

As I said before, that same principle is true for those who want to restore the joy back to their salvation. We have to put some effort behind it and keep working it, not getting surprised if some crusty old things come to the surface at first! Sometimes we have lost the joy in our salvation because we have packed our spiritual wells (hearts) with many things from this earth. They aren't necessarily bad things, but nevertheless they can hinder or clog up our spiritual pursuit.

I want you to take a moment to reflect and ask yourself what may be stopping the spiritual flow in your life. Is it Spiritual A.D.D.? Ask yourself, *What things am I neglecting in my spiritual life? Is it going to church regularly, reading my Bible, praying, or hanging with Christian friends? Have I lost the joy that should be found in my salvation?* Whatever it is, it could be what is contributing to your struggle with Spiritual A.D.D.

If we take a close look at our spiritual lives, we usually find something that is trying to stop our spiritual flow. A good way for us to get a better understanding of things stopping the flow of God in our lives is to consider a garden hose flowing powerfully with water. There is such a steady flow until something stops the flow of water. After further examination, we discover that this garden hose, which once flowed freely, now has a kink in it which is stopping the flow of water. Worse yet, it's building up pressure! This happens in our spiritual lives when dealing with Spiritual A.D.D. Things may be flowing beautifully until we allow the symptoms of Spiritual A.D.D. to cause a spiritual kink, stopping the joy and excitement that comes with serving God.

This same analogy can also apply to a well that holds water, but the water is full of dirt. The only things we could draw from it would be dirty water or no water at all, depending upon how much dirt was clogging the well. This is exactly what happened with Isaac in the Bible. He had to unclog the natural wells that his father, Abraham, had made.

> *And Isaac digged again the wells of water, which they had digged in the days of Abraham his father; for the Philistines had stopped them after the death of Abraham...* (Genesis 26:18).

They were clogged because they were full of dirt or things of this earth that the Philistines used to stop up these wells.

> *For all the wells which his father's servants had digged in the days of Abraham his father, the Philistines had stopped them, and filled them with earth* (Genesis 26:15).

Notice what the Philistine used to stop the flow of water from these wells? They filled them with earth or dirt. The dirt was now a barrier from receiving the benefits from these wells.

Just as Isaac had to unclog the wells before he could get water from them, the same is true if we are going to gain victory over Spiritual A.D.D. We will have to get the dirt, sin, and things from this earth out from clogging our spiritual wells. When our spiritual wells are clogged with worldliness or too many natural things, it makes it harder for our spiritual lives to flow. This is why people struggle with Spiritual A.D.D. and lose the joy of their salvation. They have too much of the things of this earth blocking the spiritual flow and the things of God. When this happens, we can start to experience blockage in our lives and begin losing our joy in spiritual things. As a result, some choose to neglect their salvation, preferring instead the things of this world.

If this is happening to you, and you are losing joy in your salvation, you need to get things flowing again! You need to be reminded that when you accepted Jesus as your Lord and Savior, you received a well within you of eternal life (see John 4:14). However, in addition to this initial experience, you have something else that will help get things flowing and aid in overcoming Spiritual A.D.D. It is a second experience after you become a Christian, which Jesus referred to as a river of living water that flows out of this same well of salvation.

He that believeth on Me, as the scripture hath said, out of his belly shall flow rivers of living water. (But this spake He of the Spirit, which they that believe on Him should receive: for the Holy Ghost was not yet

— 179 —

given; because that Jesus was not yet glorified) (John 7:38-39).

The Lord was referring in this verse to a second experience after salvation called the infilling or the baptism of the Holy Spirit. It's a river of power available that flows out of you when you are filled with His Spirit and then pray in the Spirit. This is such a powerful tool in your hands to get things flowing again in your life and to help you return to the joy of your salvation! This is especially true if you are feeling the effects of Spiritual A.D.D. or just plain feeling rusty like an old water pump. If this sounds like you, then I encourage you that it's time for you to begin priming your pump and get things flowing again in your walk with God!

Let me remind you of how to get things flowing again and let this river of power flow out of you. I am certain it will make it hard for Spiritual A.D.D. to latch on to your life or for you to lose that precious joy of your salvation! If you are ever struggling with your prayer life or don't feel like praying, you can spend extra, targeted time praying in the Spirit. Praying in the Spirit will build you up spiritually. *"But ye, beloved, building up yourselves on your most holy faith, praying in the Holy Ghost"* (Jude 20). Like this verse says, if you feel spiritually weak, God has made something available to build you up, to get things flowing again in your life.

Praying in the Spirit is so powerful because it is like recharging your spiritual battery, especially when natural things are draining you. If you are struggling with Spiritual A.D.D. or losing the joy of your salvation, then let me encourage you with something. How about doing a small exercise that will go a long way for you? Try praying in the Spirit for five minutes—putting your whole spirit, soul, and body into it for those five minutes. Do this every day until you are ready to increase the time. Maybe the next week you increase the time to 10 minutes. The key is changing it up and increasing it until a steady flow begins to happen in your Christian life. You will notice a difference! Are you ready to take time to exercise? If you do, you will see that it will keep you from neglecting your salvation, and it thwarts Spiritual A.D.D. as well. Watch how your hunger for the Lord increases and joy returns to your salvation. It's time to get things flowing again!

Develop Spiritual Hunger

Sometimes we are losing the joy of our salvation because Spiritual A.D.D. is causing us to lose our spiritual hunger. When this happens, we start losing our appetite for spiritual things. We can even sometimes start craving other things that may not be good for us and can even add spiritual heaviness to us.

SPIRITUAL A.D.D.

So what do you do if this is you? Well, for starters, you need to start a spiritual eating plan, so to speak, that gets your spiritual hunger and appetite back. One way you can do this is to set the Lord before you. *"I have set the LORD always before me: because He is at my right hand, I shall not be moved"* (Ps. 16:8).

In other words, you set and make a special place for Him like you would an honored guest. Something I have done in my devotions is to literally have a place set for the Lord to come meet with me. I am not intending to sound strange here but rather to mention something that will bring joy back to your salvation. I have designated at times a special chair for the Lord, and I speak to Him as if He was sitting right there in front of me. At some moments when I have done this, my whole prayer meeting place has become electrified with His presence. I want to encourage you to find what works for you. The key is to make the Lord real to you! Maybe try setting a special place for the Lord like I did. The first place to always set the Lord before you is in your heart!

When you set the Lord before you, the results will be visibly evident; you will see the joy return in your salvation, and you will start getting hungry for God again. Setting the Lord before you is a great way to keep from losing the joy of your salvation. It also helps you develop better spiritual eating habits that promote spiritual hunger. The more you feed on something, the more you will crave it. This is true in the things of God as well. The more you feed on the things of God, the hungrier you will be toward Him, and the more you will crave spiritual things.

This has happened to me when I have gone on a diet. I cut out sweets and only ate things that are nutritious. The problem is, for a period of time, my appetite and taste buds craved sugar, and the things that are better for me seemed like torture, tasting terrible! Most of the time, I had been feeding on sweets and neglecting healthy foods. I had trained my body to like sweets and to hunger for less nutritious foods. I essentially acquired a taste for sugar over nutritious things!

The same principle is true in spiritual things. Our loss of spiritual hunger can also be what keeps us from having a spiritual breakthrough. Feeding on the wrong things causes us to lose our spiritual hunger. When we do not feed on spiritual things, we lose our spiritual appetite and only desire to feed on things of the flesh. How can we increase our spiritual hunger if we feel like we are losing it to Spiritual A.D.D.? Here are some helpful things to consider in a spiritual hunger plan.

How to Develop Spiritual Hunger

1. **Go on a spiritual diet**—It requires a change of mind and heart. *"Be not conformed to this world: but be ye transformed by the renewing of*

your mind…" (Rom. 12:2). When you do, your hunger changes!

2. **Get rid of junk food and your sweet tooth, and control your cravings**—This could be, spiritually speaking, things in this world that you keep craving for that you need to do without. *"Love not the world…"* (1 John 2:15).

3. **Change your meal options, and be disciplined in what you're eating**—Choose to feed on spiritual things rather than overeating on the things in this world (see Gal. 5:16).

4. **Develop consistency and discipline in your spiritual diet**—Plan the times when you will feed on God's Word and at the Lord's table.

5. **Be accountable to others in your spiritual meal plan**—Eat with the Body of Christ through communion, fellowship, prayer, and the things of God (see Acts 2:42,46).

6. **Prioritize and simplify your life**—Stick to your spiritual meal plan by getting rid of unnecessary weight, and be diligent to exercise your spirit, seeking first the things of God (see Matt. 6:33).

7. **Keep an eye on the prize**—Keep a good attitude and be thankful, staying focused on your ultimate goal of a successful walk with God and new hunger for Him (see Col. 3:2; Isa. 55:1-3).

8. **Return to your first love**—Developing spiritual hunger requires going back to the days of your first love with the Lord and doing the things that caused you to stay hungry for Him (see Rev. 2:4).

9. **Go a little further**—Push yourself to change your spiritual eating habits. Set small goals and make small changes (see Mark 14:15).

10. **Feed on God and His Word everyday**—Develop a daily routine of prayer and reading the Word of God, working at your salvation (see Phil. 2:12).

So, how about it? Did you find this spiritual hunger plan a challenge? Are you ready to get things flowing again in your spiritual life and get that hunger back that you once had for the Lord? Have you decided it's time to go on a diet that consists of spiritual things? If you have, then you are heading in the right direction to overcome Spiritual A.D.D. in your life and return to the joy of your salvation!

Changing Direction

In order for us to successfully defeat Spiritual A.D.D. and return to lives full of the joy of our salvation, we will have to be willing to stop for a moment, catch our breath, and examine our spiritual direction and motives. This may require us to change our direction. This is true for some who may be dealing with Spiritual A.D.D. and feel like they are going in a spiritual cycle, a circle in which they will never reach their desired spiritual destination. This can leave them with a lonely and lost feeling that may persist for a long time.

This sounds like what happened to my wife and me when we were traveling through Dallas/Fort Worth on our honeymoon and were desperately lost. This newly married couple wasn't feeling very joyful because we drove around that city the whole day. Seriously, for the whole day we drove around lost! This was due to many factors. First, I refused to ask directions because I thought I knew the map. Second, I forgot my wallet when we stopped at a place in Dallas and had to drive back from Fort Worth to get it. Third, we kept taking the wrong turns, going in a never-ending circle, which made us visibly upset and frustrated! We were wandering aimlessly in the city and needed to change our direction the whole day. The directions called for us to go north, but we kept going east to west and west to east. We were not getting anywhere!

This story of our honeymoon trip reminds me of the children of Israel, who also needed to change their direction and go north. In order for them to do this, they needed to turn around and get back on the proper path. They were wandering aimlessly in the desert, circling a mountain. The Lord finally had to tell them to stop going around the same mountain, called Seir. *"You have circled this mountain long enough. Now turn north"* (Deut. 2:3 NASB). God told them they had to change their direction and head north. Why north? Prophetically speaking, it was pointing them in the direction of God's throne.

Lucifer, the devil, before he fell, drew attention to the location where God is seated, which is in the north, or the Heavens (see Isa. 14:13). The north also speaks prophetically of looking to God as our focus and not wandering in circles in our spiritual lives. The children of Israel's problem was that they got comfortable with the mountain where God had visited them all those years before. They became so familiar with it, in fact, that God told them to change it up. They were losing their first love by looking to something else. They started murmuring, complaining, and losing the joy of their salvation, which God gave them in delivering them from Egypt.

Spiritual A.D.D. works the same way. It gets you off course, and you start just maintaining, wandering, with the feeling of not reaching your desired destination, like the children of Israel. God wanted to be their focus and love. He didn't want them to just live in a mountaintop experience, all the while not really knowing Him.

As silly as it seems, like my wife and I in Dallas and the children of Israel in the wilderness, we can all wander in our spiritual lives aimlessly and foolishly because of Spiritual A.D.D. We can all get stuck in a rut spiritually and go around the same problem again and again. We start spinning our spiritual wheels, not accomplishing much, and we even start losing the joy of our salvation. Some get stuck trying to hold on to a spiritual moment or experience of the past without the joy of one in the present.

This is what happened to the children of Israel. They were holding on to their spiritual experience—when God came down on the mountain to visit them (see Exod. 19:16-20)—but they were not fulfilling their spiritual journey to enjoy and take hold of what God had promised them. So they got used to going around in circles, wandering in the desert, and not going really anywhere. This wasn't the only time in Israel's history that they got stuck. Others lost the joy of their salvation through God's deliverance from Egypt and wicked Pharaoh (see Num. 11:1-10; 14:1-4; 21:4). Some wanted to go back to Egypt, and they started complaining, getting mad, feeling frustrated, and wanting to quit. They began losing the joy of what God had and would give them.

We have to be careful we don't become like the children of Israel—mad, frustrated, complaining, and wanting to quit in our spiritual journeys. This is why God told them to go northward, and it is why He's telling us to do the same. If we really want to get serious about Spiritual A.D.D. and returning to the joy of our salvation, then we have to get determined about not going around in circles, spinning our wheels, but going nowhere spiritually. We have to be determined to change our habits, routines, and ways.

This can be difficult the older we get in life, not only physically, but also spiritually. We become resistant to change, advice, or anything that goes against what we believe and how we have always done things. The problem is we can become stagnant and determined that we aren't going to change, even if we know we should. We then often deny there is a problem, just so we can be right, and we hold on to our stubborn ways that aren't working and yielding much result in our spiritual lives and time with God.

If this sounds like you, then I think it's time to go northward. How about you?

Changing Your Habits

If we want to change our direction to restore the joy back to our salvation, then we have to be willing to change our habits. Brenda and I were lost the whole day in Dallas/Fort Worth because it is my habit not to ask for directions unless I absolutely have to. My refusal to adjust my habit affected me; I stubbornly refused to change my direction. I kept thinking I would just figure it out on my own, and I wound up losing my joy in the process!

If we really want to resist Spiritual A.D.D., then we have to be willing to change our habits. When we do, our spiritual lives will start heading in the right direction, and we will find joy again. If we want to change our habits, we must first examine our daily routines. They usually set our day and determine the course of our lives. Changing our habits will require a change in our daily routines and, at times, even our personal comfort. If we are suffering from Spiritual A.D.D., it could be because some old habits in our lives need to change.

We need to ask ourselves such questions as: *How much of my daily routine consists of a pursuit of God? Am I a Christian testimony? Do I witness to others about the Lord, or am I often too embarrassed to let anyone know I am a Christian? Are Bible reading and prayer a part of my daily habits?* These questions are important because the things we choose to do daily often lead to daily mindsets, which ultimately lead to a lifestyle from the habits that we have created. These habits can be good or bad, spiritual or unspiritual.

We can see how important it is to set the right habits in our lives daily by looking at an example of a man in the Bible who was born crippled. Every day this man was brought by others and laid down to beg at a gate called Beautiful. It became his habit, mindset, and eventually his lifestyle.

> *...A man lame from birth was being carried in. Each day he was put beside the Temple gate, the one called the Beautiful Gate, so he could beg from the people going into the Temple* (Acts 3:2 NLT).

This resulted in him having a continued life of begging for a daily handout and needing a physical healing. His daily routine formed a mindset and habit in his life. Outside of a miracle, he would stay the same for the rest of his life. The same result can happen for those who refuse to change their habits to become more spiritual and consistent. We can be left in a spiritually lame condition.

The beggar was physically lame, begging and unable to leap, dance, and worship God like he wanted to—until he was healed—because of a daily habit and mindset that hindered him. This is because he was more comfortable with his daily habits, routines, and mindsets that kept him begging for money instead of looking for an opportunity to be healed. This is why Peter said, *"Silver and gold have I none; but such as I have I give thee: in the name of Jesus Christ of Nazareth rise up and walk"* (Acts 3:6).

SPIRITUAL A.D.D.

Maybe we are like this man, who needed to change his daily habits to bring the joy he needed in his life. He needed a physical healing and a life that didn't require begging.

How do you change your daily habits to overcome Spiritual A.D.D.? First, you need to examine your routine. Is it working? Is it producing godly, productive fruit in your life? How do you start your day? Does it consist of seeking God first? This is important because what you choose to do at the start of your day will affect the rest of your day and even your life. This is why the Bible speaks so much about the importance of seeking God first thing in the morning (see Ps. 63:1; Isa. 26:9). What you prioritize first in your day is the foundation that everything else is built on.

For example, if you get up in the morning and practically smash your alarm clock as it rings for the umpteenth time, mumbling and grumbling about how tired you are and how much you hate having to start your day and go to work, this attitude will carry over in your outlook and affect the rest of your day. If you let this happen, you will find that you won't have much joy in your salvation, let alone life. How much better do you think your life would be or how much more joy would you have in your spiritual life if you would wake up with a good attitude and start your day by meeting with the Lord? What a difference it would make!

If we want to improve the joy of our salvation, then we need to ask ourselves what we are looking to receive in life. In other words, what is our motive, and what do we want to accomplish in our daily walk with the Lord? We see this in the example of the man at the gate Beautiful who daily had his eyes on the wrong thing. His eyes weren't on the Lord. His motive was not to receive a miracle but to receive money and try to make a living. There's nothing wrong with making a living, but he had his priorities wrong. His first motive and focus was not on spiritual things but rather on his daily routine of begging, which kept him in his current state. He had developed daily habits that weren't helping him to change his current situation.

Developing right habits is important if we want to see significant change. This is especially true when dealing with Spiritual A.D.D. because we can start to feel pretty low and unworthy. We may feel spiritually weak and begin having a hard time keeping our joy. When this happens, it is a good idea to examine our lives. Are we really trying to develop good habits in our lives that will help us, or are we holding onto habits that are hurting us?

Good habits are vitally important. The Lord Jesus had good habits when He walked on this earth. He sought His Heavenly Father daily, seeking Him all hours of the day, staying in constant fellowship with Him. He also had a habit of attending regular worship services (see Luke 4:16). The Bible says it was "His custom," or habit, to attend regularly.

Some struggle with their spiritual walk and Spiritual A.D.D. because they haven't developed good habits to restore the joy they need in their salvation. This is usually due to a lack of regular attendance in a good, Bible-feeding and Bible-believing church. Sometimes, it can be because they seldom choose to spend time with quality believers who can strengthen their Christian walk.

> *Let us not give up meeting together, as some are in the habit of doing, but let us encourage one another—and all the more as you see the Day approaching* (Hebrews 10:25 NIV).

Fellowshipping with other believers is important because sometimes we need others to help carry us in our Christian walk until we can get on our feet again. Getting around the right godly people who can help to restore the joy in our salvation is helpful. We may, at some point in our lives, need someone to carry us because we can't carry ourselves. The beggar at the gate Beautiful was carried daily to the gate. It's important to have people from time to time to help carry us, but we have to be careful that we don't become dependent upon them more than the Lord or make this a daily habit. We also can't use people as a spiritual crutch, never truly learning or trying to walk upright on our own.

It's good to ask ourselves what we are dependent on that we think we can't live without. It will help us to determine if we are growing or just maintaining in our spiritual walk. It will also help us to identify what could be causing bad habits in us.

For example, we often think we can't live without television or the cell phone for one night, or we depend on others to carry us in our daily habits with God. Technology is fine, and so is looking to others to help us grow in the Lord, as long as we keep these things in proper order and balance. Keeping in balance still comes back to the decisions we make as to what is most important in our day to have a successful Christian walk that values God above all else. What manner of Christians do we want to be? Do we want to live our Christian faith constantly dependent on others, looking for handouts and living in a state of spiritual lameness? Do we really want to be resistant to change and neglect our salvation? How much longer do we want to continue in the never-ending cycle of getting nowhere in our spiritual journeys?

If you are answering these questions and feeling stirred in your heart, then praise God; it means you are ready to see change! Something is happening in your spiritual walk similar to what happened to the man at the gate Beautiful. He was being changed by the supernatural power of God, which came and interrupted his daily habits and caused him to rise up healed! He became a new person, full of joy, dancing, leaping, and praising God! If that sounds like something you want, then get ready, stand to your feet, and receive the spiritual strength to walk strong again and receive joy again in your salvation!

Chapter Seven

IT WILL WORK THIS TIME

Therefore, behold, I will proceed to do a marvellous work among this people, even a marvellous work and a wonder... (Isaiah 29:14).

"What's on Your heart, God?" I asked, as I started my time of prayer with Him. I deeply wanted to know what I could do for the Lord. Was there any song He wanted me to sing to Him? Was there anything He wanted to talk to me about? I didn't come to ask Him for anything, except to know what was on His heart. You see, so often we can suffer from Spiritual A.D.D. because, rather than spend time with God developing our friendship with Him, we make the time primarily about what we can receive from Him.

If we put pressure on ourselves to have to accomplish something, rather than to develop intimacy with God, most of our spiritual pursuit will be aimed at receiving "from" God rather than ministering "to" God. We often focus primarily on our needs and our "what we need God to give us" mentality. Here's an example of what I call the "give me" mentality.

The Abram Mentality
or the Abram Response

This "give me" mentality was found in a man named Abram, who later had his name changed by the Lord to Abraham. God came to introduce Himself to Abram, who didn't know Him.

> *After these things the word of the LORD came unto Abram in a vision, saying, Fear not, Abram: I am thy shield, and thy exceeding great reward* (Genesis 15:1).

Notice in the next verse what Abram's first response was. It is often our response as well: *What will You give me?*

> *And Abram said, LORD God, what wilt Thou give me, seeing I go childless, and the steward of my house is this Eliezer of Damascus?* (Genesis 15:2)

There's nothing wrong with asking Him for things, but if God had just appeared to us, introducing Himself, would the first thing we say to Him be, "What will You give me?" It sounds kind of selfish. I am not suggesting that asking God for things is selfish but rather that our greater purpose is to love and fellowship with Him first. God desires us to make Him our focus and priority, not just what we can receive from Him, even though He wants to bless us.

That day when I asked God what was on His heart, I realized how much He wanted to bless me after that time of prayer. My focus as I went into prayer and my determination was that I wasn't going to ask God for a thing for me. Instead, I just wanted to know what I could do for Him. I asked Him what was on His heart, what He wanted to discuss. God responded by speaking to my heart about how much I blessed Him that day in being sensitive to His heart. We often forget that God is a person. He has feelings like us. He has things on His heart that He wants to discuss.

When it comes to our prayer time and our relationship with God, if we are not sensitive to the Lord's heart and needs, we will spend most of our time asking God for things rather than desiring to fellowship with Him. When we do this, we limit Him from having a chance to open up His heart to us. Please don't misunderstand me. God does want to bless us, and He enjoys it. He did tell us to ask and promised that we would receive (see Matt. 7:7-8). However, my heart is that we should be more sensitive and understanding to the Lord and

His heart. We often base most of our relationship and its success on how many things we can ask God for and receive of Him.

Abraham's first interaction with God, when he was still called Abram, was one of receiving. God was introducing Himself and getting ready to establish a covenant with him. Yet receiving was on Abram's mind instead, as is obvious in his first response to the Lord. In His introduction, the Lord did mention that He was and would be Abram's provider and compensator. *"...Fear not, Abram, I am your Shield, your abundant compensation, and your reward shall be exceedingly great"* (Gen. 15:1 AMP). Abram asked God immediately what he could receive— we might all do the same. Yet, there is something more, and it is found not just in asking God for things all the time, but in seeking and loving Him as our highest priority and focus.

After His initial introduction, God continued to bless Abram and then changed his name to Abraham and established a covenant with him (see Gen. 17). We know that Abraham became a friend to God as well because God came to discuss His heart with His friend Abraham about the future of the cities of Sodom and Gomorrah. The Lord waited to talk and discuss it with someone who would listen and be His friend. The person God found was Abraham. *"The LORD said, 'Shall I hide from Abraham what I am about to do'"* (Gen. 18:17 NASB). God wanted to discuss with him what was on His heart.

All Abraham needed to do was make himself available to fellowship with the Lord about it. If He seeks us out like that, it says something about our walk with God!

Like Abraham, we can overcome our pasts and become a friend to God. Our relationship with God will work if we make a habit of seeking God as our highest priority. He will respond by meeting our needs even before we ask! Putting Him first is also an important practice that will defeat Spiritual A.D.D. and keep it from taking hold of our time with God or spiritual endeavors. If we try to really prioritize intimacy with God, we will defeat Spiritual A.D.D. It will really work this time because God will be more actively involved in our lives and will cause our lives to come into proper order and blessing. It is a whole lot easier to avoid procrastination, tiredness, distractions, a wandering mind, and other Spiritual A.D.D. symptoms when our most important focus is ministering to God first.

When our hearts are truly dedicated and committed to being with Him and ministering to Him first, we don't feel the pressure to accomplish some spiritual routine (which is commonly subject to Spiritual A.D.D. instead of spiritual life, which focuses first on just being with God). This freedom develops our spiritual hunger and pushes aside any symptom of Spiritual A.D.D. that may be trying to affect us. It renews spiritual intimacy between us and the Lord, making seeking Him easier and more rewarding. We develop an inner fire or stirring that we would rather be with God than anything else—and that is so vital in overcoming Spiritual A.D.D.

I want to share another time with God that changed me and has been a constant reminder to me of the importance of intimacy with the Lord first and not just a "give me" mentality. On that day I went into my time with the Lord again determined not to ask God for a thing but rather to worship Him non-stop instead. I told Him I hadn't come for anything except to just be with Him.

As I continued in my worship and fellowship with God that morning, something amazing happened: He spoke back to me. After I spent some time in worship and talking with Him, asking questions and waiting for His response, He spoke into my heart. He said, "Hank, what can I bless you with?" I know He wants to bless us, but that was not what this time was to be about. In response, I kept telling the Lord that I didn't want anything. I told Him I didn't come for any other purpose but just to be with Him. What did He do? He kept insisting on wanting to bless me because my desire to just be with Him had touched Him. He, of course, already knew what I wanted and what was on my heart. His desire to bless is just so much His nature! I believe it was the motive of my heart and actions that got His attention. Well, I am no dummy. Even though it wasn't my plan to ask for anything but just to worship Him, I took Him up on His repeated offer to bless me! I began to let Him know some things I desired, and it wasn't too long until those desires were fulfilled.

Now I frequently spend time with God worshiping Him and not asking to receive anything. When I do, it seems as if God is waiting to be with me the moment I step into my prayer room. I don't feel the distractions, the feeling of tiredness, the fidgeting, and lack of focus because something has been developed in me. I am certainly not suggesting that every time I spend time with God is without spiritual pursuit or the need to discipline my spirit, soul, and body. However, the majority of the time, it is a spiritual life that really works. I am not struggling as often—through over 25 years of serving God—with staying focused and being controlled by the symptoms of Spiritual A.D.D.

I have noticed that the more I just focus on my friendship with God and worship of Him, the more blessed I am and the less the symptoms of Spiritual A.D.D. can affect my life. His presence, His love, and a disciplined life of being with Him keep Spiritual A.D.D. from taking hold. The same will be true for you! God loves friendship and fellowship, and He enjoys our time. Have you ever noticed how much Jesus took Peter, James, and John with Him to pray and do other things? I believe the Lord loved fellowship with them. Yet, I think there was also something special they had with the Lord that holds a principle that works in our lives to overcome Spiritual A.D.D.

The Peter, James, and John Principle

We can learn a powerful principle from a pattern that Jesus established in His life, which works well to combat Spiritual A.D.D. On many occasions, He took with Him three of His disciples—namely Peter, James, and John—while he didn't include the other disciples. Why did He allow only these three and not others in many of these experiences? I believe it had something to do with their prophetic purposes and destinies. We can see this in the definitions of their names. Let's look at the Greek names of these three, Peter, James, and John, as well as their prophetic meanings. We can learn from these names some powerful prophetic applications that we can apply in our spiritual lives today to help us overcome Spiritual A.D.D.

1. *Peter (Simon)*— His original name was *Simon bar Jonah.* Jesus renamed him *Peter,* or *Petros* in the Greek, meaning "a rock."

- *Prophetic application*—If we want to defeat Spiritual A.D.D., then we need to get around people who are rock solid in their faith and their walk with God. Peter also was given the keys of the Kingdom after a Kingdom revelation that Jesus was the Christ (see Matt. 16:18-19). This means we need to be around people who are Kingdom-minded also.

2. *James*—He was the brother of John. His name in the Greek is actually *Iakobos*, or *Yaakob* in the Hebrew, which means "heel-catcher or supplanter." This meaning of the name James here in the New Testament is the same as *Jacob* in the Old Testament. Jacob also wrestled with God in Scripture (see Gen. 32).

• Prophetic application—To overcome Spiritual A.D.D., it is helpful to be surrounded by those who are spiritually determined, like Jacob was when he wrestled with God. This name definition of James/Jacob prophetically speaks of the need to be around people who can pray, intercede, and break through and who are godly. Their spiritual pursuit and determination can spark something in our spiritual lives to help us succeed.

3. *John*—He was the brother of James and one of the "sons of thunder." His name in the Greek means "Yahweh is gracious." So, John is the gracious one. He is also the one who was seen leaning on Jesus' chest at the last supper.

• *Prophetic application*—Having people who are close to the heart of Jesus, like John was and like his name prophetically represents, helps us to add spiritual strength in our lives if we are dealing with Spiritual A.D.D. We need people who know God's heart and who are intimate with Him, as John's name prophetically indicates, as part of our lives to encourage us and help us grow in God's grace.

Now that we have discovered the meaning of their names and their prophetic applications, let's see what else we can prophetically glean from these three in regard to our spiritual life with God. Here is what we can conclude from Peter, James, John, and the meaning of their names.

If we are going to overcome Spiritual A.D.D. in our lives and get things working again, then we are going to need to get around godly people who have these kinds of characteristics. For example, it is important to have people who are like Peter's name definition and what he prophetically represents. They bring a dimension of rock solid Christianity to our spiritual lives. They also understand Kingdom principles and live by them, helping to bring spiritual stability to those they are around.

Surrounding ourselves with people like what Jacob prophetically represents is also vital for overcoming Spiritual A.D.D. We may need, from time to time, people who can pray, break through, and intercede to help us defeat it in our lives—people who will encourage us to keep seeking God no matter what we face.

Finally, we need people in our lives who will be like what John prophetically represents. It is important to have those who know how to hear from God and are intimate with Him in their Christian walk. We find it both refreshing and helpful to be connected to those who lean on the heart of Jesus like John did.

These prophetic applications from these names are vital for our spiritual walk today. Like the old saying says, "We are the company we keep." Thus, it is helpful to have, prophetically speaking, a "Peter," a "James," and a "John" around us. We need those who can encourage us, pray for us, take us back to the Word of God, and help us to become more intimate with the Lord. Solid Christians (Peter), those who know how to pray and break through (James), and those who know and pursue God's heart (John) will be three powerful pillars of strength in our spiritual lives!

What these names represent is a spiritual three-fold cord that won't be broken. Paul even referred to these three men as pillars to him and the Church as well. *"In fact, James, Peter, and John, who were known as pillars of the church, recognized the gift God had given me..."* (Gal. 2:9 NLT).

It helps having these sorts of people around when you are struggling in prayer or need someone to help get you going again in your Christian walk. I believe Jesus knew the powerful benefits of having others whom you can draw spiritual strength and encouragement from. This is why He brought the disciples with Him to pray in the Garden of Gethsemane just before His crucifixion (see Mark 14:32-42). He wanted to receive strength from them. This is why He asked Peter, James, and John to go a little farther from the other disciples and pray with Him. However, they fell asleep on Him three times, and Jesus couldn't count on them for help. As much as you need prayer partners or those who help to encourage you spiritually, sometimes you may not be able to count on them, or they may not be readily available. As with Jesus, it really comes down to your own pursuit and attitude to press through no matter what you are facing or feeling.

You might be thinking that you don't have anyone that you feel you can count on. Ask God to bring some people into your life; even better, you rise up and keep pursuing like Jesus did! I want you to be encouraged because God didn't leave you without hope. Don't get down if you don't have anyone yet to spiritually encourage you. It just means that you can obtain spiritually what these three names prophetically mean in your life for yourself, whether you have people or not. You can become that solid Christian like Peter. You can grow to a level of spiritual fervency and determination like James. You can have that spiritual intimacy and hear God's voice like John. Are you encouraged? See, again God didn't leave you with out hope! You can grab hold of these same prophetic pillars for yourself and stand strong and victorious as you determine to press forward to have them working in your Christian life! You really can stand upright with Jesus. In addition, He will bring others along your path in various ways to help you stand strong. You just need to be faithful to keep doing your part, and God will be faithful to do His!

Restoring the Cutting Edge

Having the right people and applying these three prophetic pillars of "Peter," "James," and "John" to our spiritual lives is an important part of reviving our spiritual lives and then staying strong spiritually.

I have learned, in the many years that I have been a Christian and in the ministry, the importance of being surrounded by the right people. I like to refer to this as the "lean on me" principle. This principle will help us to overcome Spiritual A.D.D. because, when we add this kind of dimension through building relationships with the right people, it becomes a pillar of strength to our lives.

In the story of the man at the gate Beautiful, we see an amazing act. After this man was healed at the gate, he did something that has prophetic significance for us. He was very grateful that he was healed, and the Bible records what he did to express it. He reached out and held on to Peter and John.

And as the lame man which was healed held Peter and John, all the people ran together unto them in the porch that is called Solomon's, greatly wondering (Acts 3:11).

What does that mean for us today? It represents that, if we have been feeling spiritually lame or low, we need to hold on to some spiritual truths that will be our source of strength and help like this man did. We need to reach out and lay a hold of spiritual things, solid biblical living, and solid Christian believers. The man held on to Peter with one arm, representing rock solid Christian faith and stability that puts the Kingdom of God first. The man also, with his other arm, held on to John, representing the ever-important need to find and hold on to things that are close to God's heart. It also speaks of the need to have people in our lives who have a true and committed walk with the Lord Jesus and are pursuing Him with all their hearts. These things will keep us from a place of spiritual lowness and lameness, propelling us instead to a rewarding life in the spirit.

Such relationships also help to keep us sharp in our walk with the Lord. This is extremely helpful for those who want to overcome Spiritual A.D.D. and remain on the "cutting edge." The cutting edge on a knife, for example, is the sharpest place on it. We need to keep our spiritual lives at their sharpest through having regular times with God and doing things that keep us from becoming dull. Restoring our razor-sharp cutting edge from a place of dullness will require making the right decisions and taking the necessary steps.

In the Bible, we find a story of someone who lost their cutting edge, literally (see 2 Kings 6:1-6). This man was chopping wood when the cutting edge or ax head detached from the handle and fell into the water. The ax head became disconnected from the handle, sank in the water, and ceased to be of use. What was worse for this person who lost his cutting edge was that this tool was borrowed! This caused him to seek the prophet Elisha for help in getting his cutting edge back.

> …*"Oh, sir!" he cried. "It was a borrowed ax!" "Where did it fall?" the man of God asked. When he showed him the place, Elisha cut a stick and threw it into the water at that spot. Then the ax head floated to the surface. "Grab it," Elisha said. And the man reached out and grabbed it* (2 Kings 6:5-7 NLT).

What a supernatural miracle for the ax head to float to the top of the water after it sank! This is amazing because iron doesn't float. What was better yet for this man, was that he was able to reconnect the cutting edge to the handle again. You could say he got a handle on things!

SPIRITUAL A.D.D.

What does this story mean for us, and how does it relate to overcoming Spiritual A.D.D.? If we feel like we our spiritual cutting edge has sunk like that ax head, we must not despair because, if God can cause an iron ax head to resurface, He can cause our spiritual lives to rise again as well! This is encouraging for those who really want to stay sharp in their Christianity or overcome Spiritual A.D.D. Rather than get upset, we need to tap into the power of God and the tools He has made available to sharpen our walk with Him. We also have to reconnect with some things that may help in restoring our "cutting edge" for the Lord.

Many spiritually sink or drift in their walk with God because they don't stay connected to the things that keep them spiritually sharp and intact, like the ax head. One way to stay sharp and not lose your cutting edge is to be thankful and to rehearse what God has done for you. Something I suggest you consider, if you want to restore that cutting edge in your spiritual life, is making a checklist of things you are believing God for. Then follow up with continual thanks and praise to the Lord for His answers. When you see the things you listed start manifesting before your eyes (and even before they do), it is important not to forget to thank the Lord and remind Him of specific answers to prayers. These things will keep you spiritually sharp and keep you from thinking that nothing is working in your spiritual life.

Here are some other suggestions to help you restore and keep your cutting edge. They will work, even if you feel like your cutting edge is sinking like the ax head. The key to remember is: *It will resurface if you believe it can!* This is what I call "restoring your cutting edge." This is not an all-inclusive list, but it includes many helpful tips:

- Prioritize your day by seeking God and putting Him first, setting a time and place to meet.

- Pray in the Spirit often every day, building yourself up to pray for longer periods of time.

- Find a strong, Bible-believing church where God's Spirit and presence are.

- Get around other strong believers (those who are like Peter, James, and John).

- Pray and meditate on the Word of God every day and night.

- Find a good Christian book, devotional, or biblical study book.

- When driving in your car, worship and pray with your understanding and in the Spirit.

- Share and be bold about your faith. Look for evangelism opportunities.

- Get involved in your local church, serving others.

- Consider a short-term mission trip.

- Learn about safe and effective fasting, as well as the biblical benefits of fasting.

- Listen to worship and praise music in your car and in your home often.

- Monitor your television, computer, and cell phone use and your other activities.

- Avoid sin, carnal people, and worldly influences.

Build an Altar

As we bring this chapter and book to a close, I believe something new is opening for you. It is a greater, more fulfilled, and more spiritually intimate life with the Lord. I pray that the principles you have learned throughout this book have challenged you—that they made you laugh and made you feel as though you could relate to the things mentioned. Yet I pray that you have also found the tools you need to inspire you to overcome Spiritual A.D.D., not letting it reign in your life!

I believe that a spark has been lit, and now a new spiritual fire is beginning to burn in you! You have gained new insights, strategies, and principles that you can apply to your spiritual walk. In the end, as you reflect on what you have read, realize that it really comes down to consistently building an altar with God every day. When you do this, you will see life spring up again in your walk with God. You will see the things that you have cried out for, and you will continue on a road to a greater depth in the things of God.

Before ending, let's take a small glimpse at the importance of a personal altar with God. Altars in the Bible were very significant, and God required many people to build them. An altar represents so much. It represents a place to meet with God and to seek His face. It represents a place of sacrifice and worship. It is a place to show your love, heart, and commitment to the Lord. An altar is a place to find forgiveness of sin and to receive a clean start again.

So how do we build a personal spiritual altar to meet with God? Let's look at an example and apply it to us today. Noah built an altar before the Lord after the flood had been on the earth. This altar represented a fresh start, a commitment to God and His covenant. It signified that things were working in the earth as God brought restoration after the flood, which had destroyed all that was in the earth except Noah and the animals in the ark.

SPIRITUAL A.D.D.

Then Noah built an altar to the LORD and, taking some of all the clean animals and clean birds, he sacrificed burnt offerings on it. The LORD smelled the pleasing aroma... (Genesis 8:20-21 NIV).

Building an altar was something that Noah did on his own to worship and honor God. It wasn't something that God necessarily commanded him to do. We can apply the same principle that Noah did to help us overcome Spiritual A.D.D. An altar is a place to meet with God and develop our spiritual walk. It is also where we present our hearts, our worship, our sacrifice, and anything else we want to present to the Lord. At this altar, Noah presented some clean animals. This means we need to present ourselves as clean vessels before the Lord. The more pure we are in our hearts, the more we will see God and the less Spiritual A.D.D. we will have in our lives (see Matt. 5:8).

Another thing we can do in building an altar is to bring our lives as an act of worship, honor, and obedience to the Lord. Notice what happens when we establish an altar. (I am not speaking of a physical altar high up on a hill with artifacts and statues or some odd shrine in some room in our home. I am speaking of our hearts and establishing a consistent time and place to be with the Lord, not some religious ritual.) When we establish a spiritual altar to the Lord, connecting our hearts and everything we are and have to Him, He responds!

The Lord responded to Noah by saying:

And the LORD smelled a sweet savour; and the LORD said in His heart, I will not again curse the ground any more for man's sake; for the imagination of man's heart is evil from his youth; neither will I again smite any more every thing living, as I have done. While the earth remaineth, seedtime and harvest, and cold and heat, and summer and winter, and day and night shall not cease (Genesis 8:21-22).

We can see the Lord's response was favorable and one of blessing to Noah and future generations. Are you hungry to build that new spiritual altar between you and the Lord like Noah did? I bet you are! I challenge you to do so and to watch how things will work for you in your walk with Jesus. You will experience an amazing God releasing amazing results in your spiritual life. Are you ready to start building?

The good thing is that I believe you have already started! You know how I know? Think for a moment! Look at how great a step you have taken by actually making it to the end of this book. That is, of course, if you didn't skip to the back and are just reading this sentence. But all joking aside! If you were dealing with the symptoms of Spiritual A.D.D. and you have read the pages of this book, then I think you need to applaud yourself (careful not to make a scene now). You have completed a great step, a necessary step to better and further your walk with God. You have actually started to build your spiritual altar before the Lord.

I am convinced you are on your way to seeing results, but don't let this stop with you. Pass this book on to someone else you know who could really benefit from it also. It is working! Just keep moving forward! Victory is on the horizon, and you are sailing right into the spiritual life you have longed for! Happy spiritual altar building; say goodbye to Spiritual A.D.D.!

●————————●

ABOUT HANK KUNNEMAN

Hank Kunneman is senior pastor of Lord of Hosts Church in Omaha, Nebraska, and founder of One Voice Ministries. Hank is known for his prophetic ministry and prophetic words for nations and world events. His prophetic Web site called *Prophetic Perspectives* has been an encouragement to many. He travels extensively, ministering in conferences and churches throughout the United States and overseas. He demonstrates the power of God and preaches biblical truths that stir the Body of Christ, while equipping people to do the work of the ministry. Hank also ministers with his wife, Brenda, and has authored several books, including *Barrier Breakers, Don't Leave God Alone,* and *The Revealer of Secrets.*

OTHER BOOKS BY HANK KUNNEMAN

The Revealer of Secrets

Don't Leave God Alone

Barrier Breakers

In the right hands, This Book will Change Lives!

Most of the people who need this message will not be looking for this book. To change their lives, you need to put a copy of this book in their hands.

> *But others (seeds) fell into good ground, and brought forth fruit, some a hundred-fold, some sixty-fold, some thirty-fold* (Matthew 13:8).

Our ministry is constantly seeking methods to find the good ground, the people who need this anointed message to change their lives. Will you help us reach these people?

> *Remember this—a farmer who plants only a few seeds will get a small crop. But the one who plants generously will get a generous crop* (2 Corinthians 9:6).

EXTEND THIS MINISTRY BY SOWING
3 BOOKS, 5 BOOKS, 10 BOOKS, OR MORE TODAY,
AND BECOME A LIFE CHANGER!

Thank you,

Don Nori Sr., Founder
Destiny Image
Since 1982

DESTINY IMAGE PUBLISHERS, INC.

*"Speaking to the Purposes of God for This Generation
and for the Generations to Come."*

VISIT OUR NEW SITE HOME AT
WWW.DESTINYIMAGE.COM

FREE SUBSCRIPTION TO DI NEWSLETTER

Receive free unpublished articles by top DI authors, exclusive

discounts, and free downloads from our best and newest books.

Visit www.destinyimage.com to subscribe.

Write to: Destiny Image
              P.O. Box 310
              Shippensburg, PA 17257-0310

Call: 1-800-722-6774

Email: orders@destinyimage.com

For a complete list of our titles or to place an order
online, visit www.destinyimage.com.

FIND US ON FACEBOOK OR FOLLOW US ON TWITTER.

www.facebook.com/destinyimage   facebook
www.twitter.com/destinyimage   twitter